COTSWOLDS TRAVEL GUIDE 2024-2025

Cotswolds' Magic: Escape to Enchantment & History

JOSE D. GILLIAM

Copyright © 2024 by Jose D. Gilliam

All rights reserved. No part of this publication may be reproduced, distributed, or transmitted in any form or by any means, including photocopying, recording, or other electronic or mechanical methods, without the prior written permission of the publisher.

TABLE OF CONTENT

TABLE OF CONTENT..3
INTRODUCTION...7
    Welcome to Cotswolds: A Land of Timeless Beauty 7
    Why Cotswolds Should Be Your Next Travel Destination...9
    Brief History of Cotswolds..11
CHAPTER 1:
GETTING STARTED..**13**
    Understanding the Essence of Cotswolds..............13
    Best Time to Visit Cotswolds..................................14
    Essential Items to Pack for Your Trip......................16
    Visa & Entry Requirements.....................................18
    Insurance Coverage..21
    Local Norm & Etiquettes...23
CHAPTER 2:
GETTING TO COTSWOLDS......................................**26**
    Soaring In: Arriving by Air..26
    Train Travel: A Scenic Journey...............................28
    Hitting the Road: A Cotswolds Road Trip...............29
CHAPTER 3:
GETTING AROUND COTSWOLDS...........................**33**
    Public Transport: Exploring on a Budget................33
    Lace Up Your Boots: Exploring the Cotswolds on Foot...35
    Renting a Car: Freedom to Roam at Your Own Pace..36
    Cycling Adventures: Pedal Through Picturesque

Landscapes.. 37

CHAPTER 4:
WHERE TO STAY 40

Luxurious Retreats: Spa Resort and Country Estate... 40

Quaint Villages: Charming Cottages and Holiday Rentals.. 42

Camping Under the Stars: Campsites and Glamping Options... 44

CHAPTER 5:
EXPLORING COTSWOLDS 47

Iconic Villages and Towns: Must-Visit Destinations 47

Historic Landmarks: Castles, Manors, and Abbeys 50

Natural Wonders: Gardens, Parks, and Nature Reserves... 53

Culinary Delights: Food and Drink Experiences in Cotswolds.. 56

CHAPTER 6:
EXPERIENCING COTSWOLDS CULTURE 58

Festivals and Events: Celebrating Local Traditions 58

Art and Craft Galleries: Showcasing Creative Talents... 65

Museums and Heritage Sites: Delving into Cotswolds' Rich History................................... 68

Engaging with Locals: Workshops, Classes, and Cultural Exchanges.................................... 70

CHAPTER 7:
INSIDER TIPS & LOCAL SECRETS 73

Off-the-Beaten-Path Spots: Secret Spots Revealed... 73

Practical Advice from Locals & Expats................... 76

CHAPTER 8:
OUTDOOR ADVENTURES.. 80
Rambling Routes: Scenic Walks and Hikes............80
Waterway Escapes: Canal Boating and River Cruises...82
Adrenaline Rush: Outdoor Activities for Thrill Seekers..84
Wildlife Encounters: Birdwatching and Nature Excursions... 87

CHAPTER 9:
PRACTICAL TIPS..90
Money Matters: Currency, Banking, and Budgeting..90
Staying connected: Wi-Fi and mobile coverage..... 91
Health and Safety: Important Precautions and Emergency Contacts.. 93
Sustainable Travel: Environmentally Friendly Practices and Responsible Tourism........................95
Further Reading..98

CHAPTER 10:
3-DAY TAILORED ITINERARIES............................. 100
The History Buff's Retreat.....................................100
Adventure seeker...101
Honeymoon Couples Escape............................... 104
Luxury Seekers..106
Family-friendly Getaway...................................... 109
Budget Traveler..111
Solo Traveler..113

CHAPTER 11:
BEYOND COTSWOLDS..116
- Day Trips and Excursions: Nearby Attractions and Hidden Gems.. 116
- Exploring Nearby Cities: Oxford, Bath, and Stratford-upon-Avon...118
- Extended Adventures: Planning Your Next Journey from Cotswolds.. 120

CHAPTER 12:
SHOPPING & SOUVENIRS.......................................124
- Unique Boutiques & Antique Stores..................... 124
- Local Products to Bring Home............................. 127

CHAPTER 13:
CLOSING THOUGHTS...130
- Tips for Preserving Memories and Sharing Your Stories...130
- Farewell to Cotswolds: Until We Meet Again........ 131

ACKNOWLEDGEMENT..133
- Special Thanks to the Locals, Experts and Contributors.. 133

INTRODUCTION

Welcome to Cotswolds: A Land of Timeless Beauty

My exploration began in Bibury, a place so gorgeous it could be a movie scene. The Arlington Row, a row of identical 17th-century cottages, mirrored perfectly in the quiet waters of the River Coln, took my breath away. I went through little alleyways, past gardens bursting with roses and lavender, feeling transported to a calmer time.

The Cotswolds aren't only about picture-perfect villages, though. I grabbed my walking boots and headed on a hike among the emerald hills. Lush fields, filled with grazing sheep, gave place to old trees, their serenity broken only by the lyrical sounds of unseen birds. The air was revitalizing, full with the earthy aroma of damp soil and the delicate perfume of wildflowers.

At the end of each day, I found myself drawn to small taverns with crackling fires and locals with stories engraved onto their faces like maps. Over pints of good ale and dishes of hearty stews, I heard about the Cotswolds' rich history, from Roman settlements to the golden age of the wool trade.

One lovely afternoon, I came upon a hidden gem - Hidcote Manor Garden. Meandering through perfectly planned flowerbeds, I marveled at the burst of colors and textures. Each portion was a gem of horticultural craftsmanship, a monument to the Cotswolds' strong relationship with nature.

As my time in the Cotswolds drew to an end, I felt a sense of sadness. But it was swiftly replaced with a warmth that flowed through me. This wasn't just a vacation; it was a homecoming to a location that resonated with my soul.

The Cotswolds aren't only about beauty, though it's definitely breathtaking. It's about a slower pace of life, a connection to the earth, and the simple delight of being present. It's a place that reminds you to breathe deeply, enjoy the little things, and savor the timeless beauty that surrounds us all.

So, if you're searching for a spot to escape the rush and bustle of modern life, the Cotswolds beckon. Come, lose yourself in its ageless appeal, and discover the magic that awaits.

Why Cotswolds Should Be Your Next Travel Destination

Craving a retreat that exceeds the ordinary? Look no further than the Cotswolds, a timeless patchwork of rolling English hills, charming villages, and genuine charm. Here's why this lovely locale should be your next holiday destination in 2024-2025:

Escape the Ordinary, Embrace the Extraordinary:

Step into a Fairytale: Imagine beautiful villages trapped in time, where honey-colored houses display overflowing flower boxes and tiny pathways whisper secrets of a bygone era. The Cotswolds isn't simply a destination; it's an experience that transports you to a universe where time slows down and calm reigns supreme.

A Breath of Fresh Air (Literally): Inhale the invigorating English countryside. Lush meadows studded with grazing sheep give way to old forests alive with life. The Cotswolds give a chance to reconnect with nature, a valuable respite from the pollution and cacophony of metropolitan life.

Beyond the Picture-perfect: The Cotswolds are more than just a collection of lovely villages. Hike across verdant hills, uncover secret waterfalls, or cycle along charming country lanes. Immerse yourself in the region's unique tapestry, from Roman remains hinting of vanished empires to medieval mansions exhibiting stunning gardens.

A Foodie's Paradise: In 2024-2025, the Cotswolds' culinary culture is flourishing. Sample local specialties like melt-in-your-mouth Cotswold cheese, luscious Gloucester pig, and a refreshing pint of real ale in cozy pubs crackling with warmth. Don't miss out on the chance to discover Michelin-starred restaurants pushing the boundaries of modern British cuisine, all drawn from the freshest local food.

Sustainable Travel: The Cotswolds are embracing sustainable practices. Many hotels and B&Bs stress eco-friendly efforts, and there's a growing emphasis on locally sourced food and responsible walking and cycling pathways. Explore the region with a clear conscience, knowing you're reducing your environmental impact.

The Cotswolds aren't merely a destination; they're an experience for the soul. So pack your luggage, lace up your walking boots, and get ready to experience a location that will stay with you long after you return home.

Brief History of Cotswolds

The Cotswolds boast a rich history spanning back millennia. Here's a whistle-stop tour:

Ancient Beginnings: Evidence supports settlements as far back as the Neolithic period, with burial chambers found on the Cotswold Edge. The Bronze and Iron Age saw the construction of spectacular hill forts, hinting at organized settlements.

Roman Flair: The Romans marched in and left their imprint, erecting villas (like the one at Chedworth) and founding settlements, including Gloucester (formerly the second-largest town in Britain!). They even paved the Fosse Way, a crucial road still utilized today.

Medieval Boom: The Middle Ages saw the birth of the Cotswolds' most famous export: wool. The region's undulating hills were suitable for sheep grazing, and the Cotswold Lion breed became famed for its lustrous fleece. This prosperity is reflected in the majestic buildings and fine mansions built by affluent wool merchants.

Civil War Stage: The 17th century saw the Cotswolds entangled in the English Civil War. The strategic location, with Oxford as Royalist headquarters and Gloucester and Bristol occupied by Parliamentarians, made it a battleground. The first encounter ever took place in Edgehill on the Cotswolds' northern edge.

A Timeless Beauty: The Cotswolds continued to adapt, but its core remained. Today, it's a declared Area of Outstanding Natural Beauty, a testimony to its continuing charm and a reflection of its rich and lively past.

CHAPTER 1:

GETTING STARTED

Understanding the Essence of Cotswolds

Before diving headfirst into crafting your Cotswolds getaway, take time to understand what truly speaks to you about this region. Here's a quick help to get you started:

Tranquility or Active Adventure: Do you crave lazy afternoons in charming villages, or are you yearning for invigorating hikes and outdoor pursuits? The Cotswolds provide both! Knowing your preference will help you select the perfect base and activities.

History Buff or Foodie at Heart: Are you fascinated by bygone eras, or does the thought of sampling local cuisines set your taste buds tingling? The Cotswolds cater to all interests. Research historical sites or acclaimed restaurants beforehand to curate a personalized itinerary.

Cozy Pubs or Michelin-Starred Fare: Imagine evenings spent in traditional pubs with crackling fires, or indulging in exquisite multi-course foods. The Cotswolds provide a spectrum of dining experiences. Consider your budget and preferences to create the perfect culinary adventure.

Village Charm or Bustling Market Towns: The Cotswolds bolsters idyllic villages like Bibury and Bourton-on-the-Water, or lively market towns like Cirencester and Tetbury. Choose an atmosphere that works for you - tranquil escape or vibrant exploration.

By understanding your travel style and interests, you can unlock the Cotswolds' essence and plan an unforgettable experience tailored just for you. Remember, the magic lies not just in the sights, but in how they connect with your soul.

Best Time to Visit Cotswolds

The best time to visit Cotswolds largely depends on your wants and what you hope to experience during your trip. However, there are a few factors to consider when crafting your visit:

1. Spring (March to May):
- Springtime in Cotswolds brings blooming flowers, lush greenery, and milder temperatures.

- It's an optimum time for outdoor activities such as hiking, cycling, and exploring the countryside.
- You'll also have the opportunity to witness lambs frolicking in the fields and gardens coming to life with unique colors.

2. Summer (June to August):
- Summer is the peak tourist season in Cotswolds, thanks to its warm weather and longer daylight hours.
- This is the perfect time for outdoor events, festivals, and al fresco dining in the enchanting villages.
- Be set for larger crowds and higher accommodation prices, especially in popular tourist spots.

3. Autumn (September to November):
- Autumn in Cotswolds is a photographer's dream, with the landscape lit in hues of red, orange, and gold as the leaves change color.
- It's a quieter time to visit compared to summer, offering a more peaceful and personal experience.
- Enjoy scenic walks through wooded areas, cozy evenings by the fireplace, and seasonal harvest festivals.

4. Winter (December to February):
- Winter brings a magical atmosphere to Cotswolds, with frost-covered landscapes and cozy villages adorned with twinkling lights.

- It's an excellent time for indoor activities such as touring historic sites, exploring museums, and indulging in hearty meals at traditional pubs.
- Keep in mind that some attractions and accommodations may have limited hours or closures during the winter months.

In essence, the best time to visit Cotswolds depends on your personal preferences, whether you like the vibrant energy of summer, the quietness of autumn, or the festive charm of winter. No matter when you choose to visit, Cotswolds promises unforgettable and enchanting experiences.

Essential Items to Pack for Your Trip

When packing for your trip to Cotswolds, it's necessary to be set for various weather conditions and outdoor adventures. Here are some essential items to consider bringing along:

1. Weather-Appropriate Clothing:
- Layered clothing for unforseen weather, including a waterproof jacket, sweaters, and suitable walking shoes.
- Sun protection such as a wide-brimmed hat, sunglasses, and sunscreen, especially in the summer months.

2. Daypack:
A sturdy backpack or daypack to carry essentials like water bottles, snacks, maps, and guidebooks while exploring the countryside.

3. Comfortable Footwear:
Comfortable walking shoes or hiking boots with good traction for traversing Cotswolds' scenic trails and cobblestone streets.

4. Camera or Smartphone:
Capture the beauty of Cotswolds with a camera or smartphone to preserve memories of your journey through picturesque villages and landscapes.

5. Reusable Water Bottle:
Stay hydrated while touring by bringing a reusable water bottle to refill at local cafes, pubs, and water fountains.

6. Travel Adapter and Charger:
A universal travel adapter and charger to keep your electronic devices powered up during your trip.

7. First Aid Kit:
A basic first aid kit with essentials like band-aids, pain relievers, antiseptic wipes, and any personal medications you may need.

8. Map or GPS Device:
A map or GPS device to explore Cotswolds' winding roads and trails, especially if you plan to explore off the beaten path.

9. Travel Guide or App:
A travel guidebook or smartphone app with information about local attractions, dining options, and points of interest.

10. Snacks and Picnic Supplies:
Pack snacks such as trail mix, granola bars, and fruit for energy during outdoor adventures, as well as a picnic blanket or portable chairs for leisurely al fresco dining.

By packing these essential items, you'll be well-prepared to embark on a memorable journey through the timeless beauty of Cotswolds, ready to traverse its charming villages, scenic countryside, and rich cultural heritage.

Visa & Entry Requirements

For first-time tourists to the Cotswolds, it's necessary to be aware of the visa and entry procedures for visiting the United Kingdom. Here are some crucial aspects to consider:

1. Visa Requirements:
- Citizens of several countries, including the United States, Canada, Australia, and members of the European Union, do not often need a visa for short visits to the UK for tourism purposes (usually up to 6 months).
- A However, visa requirements may vary depending on your nationality, duration of stay, and the purpose of your travel. It's vital to check the UK government's official website or call the nearest British embassy or consulate in your country for the most up-to-date information on visa requirements.
- A If you are unsure if you need a visa, or if you want to stay longer than the visa-free period allows, it's advisable to apply for a visa well in advance of your trip.

2. Entry Requirements:
- All passengers to the UK must have a valid passport with at least six months' validity left beyond the intended term of stay.
- Additionally, passengers may be asked to produce proof of adequate finances to cover their stay, a return or onward ticket, and accommodation details.
- Upon arrival in the UK, tourists may undergo immigration inspections, including biometric scans and interviews with border officers.

3. Electronic Travel Authorization (ETA):

- Some tourists, notably those from visa-exempt countries, may be required to get an Electronic Travel Authorization (ETA) before traveling to the UK. This online authorization permits people to enter the nation without a visa for short visits.
 - A The official website for applying for an ETA for the UK is: www.gov.uk/check-uk-visa

4. COVID-19 Travel Restrictions:
- Due to the current COVID-19 pandemic, travel restrictions and entrance criteria may be subject to change at short notice. It's crucial to keep updated about any travel advisories or health laws in force at the time of your trip.
- Travelers should consult the UK government's official website and relevant health authorities for the latest information on COVID-19 travel restrictions and entrance procedures.

Before going on your trip to the Cotswolds, be sure to investigate and familiarize yourself with the visa and entry procedures appropriate to your nationality. By preparing early and ensuring you have the proper papers, you may enjoy a seamless and hassle-free vacation experience in this beautiful region of the United Kingdom.

Insurance Coverage

For first-time tourists to Cotswolds, buying travel insurance is strongly suggested to ensure peace of mind and protection against unforeseen incidents. Here are some crucial factors to consider regarding insurance coverage:

1. Medical Coverage:
- Travel insurance should include comprehensive medical coverage, including covering for medical crises, hospitalization, and medical evacuation if necessary.
- Ensure that the policy covers pre-existing medical issues, as well as any activities you want to participate in, such as hiking or cycling.

2. Trip Cancellation and Interruption:
- Look for a policy that covers coverage for trip cancellation and interruption due to unforeseen situations, such as illness, injury, or natural disasters.
- This coverage can compensate you for non-refundable charges, such as airfare, lodgings, and tour bookings, if your vacation is canceled or cut short.

3. Baggage and Personal possessions:
- Choose a policy that covers coverage for lost, stolen, or damaged baggage and personal possessions, including

valuable things such as electronics, cameras, and jewelry.

- Be sure to verify the policy limits and exclusions to ensure they match your needs.

4. Travel aid Services:
Look for a policy that offers travel aid services, such as 24/7 emergency assistance hotlines, travel concierge services, and assistance with rebooking flights or lodgings in case of crises.

5. COVID-19 Coverage:
- Given the ongoing COVID-19 pandemic, consider acquiring a policy that offers coverage for COVID-related expenses, such as medical treatment, quarantine accommodation, and travel cancellation due to COVID-related reasons.
- Check with insurance providers for particular specifics on COVID-19 coverage and any exclusions connected to pandemics.

Recommended Insurance Websites:
-World Nomads: www.worldnomads.com
-Allianz Travel: www.allianztravelinsurance.com
-Travel Guard: www.travelguard.com

Before getting travel insurance, carefully research the policy coverage, exclusions, and terms and conditions to verify it suits your unique needs and offers appropriate protection for your trip to Cotswolds. Having comprehensive travel insurance can provide vital support and help in case of emergencies or unforeseen incidents during your travels.

Local Norm & Etiquettes

Understanding local conventions and etiquette is vital for first-time travelers to Cotswolds to ensure a respectful and pleasurable experience. Here are some fundamental conventions and manners to bear in mind while visiting:

1. Politeness and civility: British society lays a significant premium on politeness and civility. Be sure to greet locals with a friendly "hello" or "good morning" and say "please" and "thank you" in interactions.

2. Queuing (Waiting in Line): British people are known for their love of queuing. Whether waiting to board a bus, enter a museum, or order meals at a pub, always join the end of the queue and wait your turn calmly.

3. Respecting Personal Space: Britons appreciate their personal space and may feel uncomfortable with excessively familiar gestures or invading personal boundaries. Maintain a polite distance when interacting with others.

4. Tipping: Tipping is not as prevalent or anticipated in the UK as it is in some other nations. In restaurants, a service charge may be included in the bill, but if not, leaving a 10-15% tip is usual for good service.

5. Pubs and Socializing: Pubs are a vital aspect of British society, and chatting over a pint is a typical pastime. When entering a pub, wait to be served at the bar and avoid raising your voice or causing a commotion.

6. Dining Etiquette: When dining out, it's customary to wait to be seated by the host or hostess. Keep elbows off the table while eating, and use utensils rather than eating with your hands unless it's suitable (e.g., fish and chips).

7. Driving and Pedestrian Etiquette:
-In the UK, cars drive on the left side of the road. Always glance right before crossing the street, as traffic comes from the right.
- When taking public transit, allow others to exit before boarding, and give up your seat to elderly or disabled passengers if needed.

8. Cultural Sensitivity: Be respectful of cultural and religious differences. Avoid making jokes or comments that could be interpreted as insulting, and be careful of dress rules when visiting religious sites or attending formal gatherings.

By adopting these local standards and etiquette, you'll not only show respect for the culture and customs of Cotswolds but also enhance your whole travel experience by creating pleasant relationships with locals and immersing yourself more thoroughly in the area.

CHAPTER 2:

GETTING TO COTSWOLDS

The Cotswolds beckon with their rolling hills, storybook villages, and timeless beauty. But before you lose yourself in its charm, you need to get there! This masterpiece analyzes your arrival alternatives, highlighting the best routes, transport links, and items to consider for a pleasant journey.

Soaring In: Arriving by Air

The Cotswolds lack a designated airport, although numerous major airports in England operate as gateways to this wonderful region. Here's how to navigate your arrival:

London Heathrow Airport (LHR): The busiest airport in Europe, Heathrow has good connectivity worldwide. However, getting a train or coach from London adds travel time and money.

Pros & Cons
Pros: Extensive flying possibilities, convenient for international travelers.

Cons: Distance from Cotswolds (about 1.5-2 hour train/coach journey), perhaps greater travel expenditures.

Birmingham Airport (BHX): Located closer to the Cotswolds (about 1-hour train travel), Birmingham offers a suitable option, especially for flights from inside Europe.

Pros & Cons
Pros: Closer proximity to Cotswolds, maybe lower travel costs.
Cons: Fewer airline alternatives compared to Heathrow.

Navigating from Airport to Cotswolds: Upon arrival, you have many options:

Trains: Direct trains connect both Heathrow and Birmingham to stations inside the Cotswolds, like Moreton-in-Marsh and Cheltenham Spa. Check National Rail: www.nationalrail.co.uk for timetables and tickets (prices vary based on route and time of booking, anticipate to pay roughly £20-£50 one-way).

Coaches: National Express coaches offer a budget-friendly option from both airports to major Cotswolds towns like Cirencester and Gloucester. Check National Express: www.nationalexpress.com for timetables and fares (prices normally start around £10-£20 one-way).

Pre-booked Car Hire: Renting a car allows maximum flexibility for exploring the Cotswolds at your own speed. Several automobile rental businesses operate at both airports.

Note: Book your onward transport (train tickets, coach tickets, or car rentals) in advance, especially during high seasons.

Train Travel: A Scenic Journey

For a more relaxing and scenic arrival, consider traveling by train. The Cotswolds are well-connected to major UK cities via the national rail network.

Highlights: Sit back, relax, and enjoy the ever-changing English scenery as you cruise into the Cotswolds.

Stations: Key stations within the Cotswolds include Moreton-in-Marsh, Cheltenham Spa, Gloucester, and Swindon. These stations link to important cities like London, Birmingham, Oxford, and Bristol.

Pricing: Train costs vary depending on the route, travel time, and booking time. Advance tickets provide great reductions, so plan ahead! Expect to pay roughly £20-£80 one-way, depending on the distance and booking time.

Pros & Cons
Pros: Scenic journey, comfortable travel experience, handy connections to major cities.
Cons: Potentially longer travel time compared to flying, restricted freedom for touring the Cotswolds (needs further connections via local buses or taxis).

Planning Your Train Journey: Use the National Rail website www.nationalrail.co.uk to search for routes, schedules, and fares. Consider obtaining a BritRail Pass if you plan on considerable train travel within the UK.

Hitting the Road: A Cotswolds Road Trip

For the utmost freedom and flexibility, embark on a road trip to the Cotswolds. The journey itself becomes part of the adventure.

Road Trip Tips:

Plan Your Route: The Cotswolds encompass multiple counties. Decide on your base town(s) and plot out scenic routes using Google Maps or Automobile Association (AA) route planner: www.theaa.com/route-planner.

Rent a Car: Choose a car that meets your needs and budget. Consider fuel efficiency, as some Cotswolds villages have limited gas station options.

Mind the Speed Limits: Speed limits vary around the UK. Be mindful of signage and change your driving accordingly.

Routes:
The Cotswolds are conveniently accessible from numerous major motorways (M4, M5). Once on smaller country roads, appreciate the quaint villages and idyllic countryside. Popular routes include:

The Cotswolds Way: A picturesque 102-mile scenic path spanning the heart of the Cotswolds. The Heart of England Way: A lengthier 200-mile path includes not simply the Cotswolds, but also the Malvern Hills and Shakespeare's Country.

Pros: Ultimate flexibility for exploring hidden gems, freedom to adjust your itinerary on the go, scenic drives through quintessentially English countryside.

Cons: Requires good navigation skills and planning, parking can be limited in some villages, traffic congestion can occur during peak seasons.

Things to Consider:

Car Rental Costs: Rental car fees vary depending on the automobile type, rental agency, and season. Budget roughly £30-£80 every day, not counting petrol expenditures.

Fuel prices: Factor in fuel prices while budgeting for your road trip. Gas costs in the UK are often higher than in the US.

Exploring the Cotswolds by automobile allows you to completely immerse yourself in its beauty. With careful planning and the correct car, your Cotswolds road trip promises to be a wonderful adventure.

The Cotswolds are eager to be discovered! Whether you prefer to soar in by air, rest on a gorgeous train journey, or embark on a self-guided road adventure, there's a suitable arrival option for you. Now that you know how to get there, start arranging your Cotswolds retreat and be ready to discover a destination that will stay with you long after you return home.

CHAPTER 3:

GETTING AROUND COTSWOLDS

The Cotswolds' splendor reveals not simply in its picture-perfect villages, but also in the delightful byways and hidden gems waiting to be discovered. This book explores several ways to navigate about the Cotswolds, ensuring you don't miss a single interesting corner.

Public Transport: Exploring on a Budget

While a car offers ultimate freedom, the Cotswolds boast a decent public transit network, allowing you to explore the region on a budget. If you want to know something, here it is:

Buses: Stagecoach operates a network of buses connecting key Cotswolds towns and villages. While timetables may be less regular than in larger cities, buses offer a budget-friendly choice for moving around: www.stagecoachbus.com.

The Robin: A new, hop-on, hop-off service named "The Robin" connects many villages in the North Cotswolds, great for exploring hidden gems without a car:
Prices: Tickets start at around £2 each travel.

Trains: Trains connect some of the main Cotswolds communities like Moreton-in-Marsh and Cheltenham Spa to major UK cities. While not the most extensive network for touring particular villages, trains offer a pleasant choice for specific travels within the Cotswolds: www.nationalrail.co.uk.

Taxis: Taxis are commonly accessible in bigger Cotswolds towns and can be a practical choice for short excursions or evenings out. However, fares can add up rapidly, so consider this for specific journeys rather than broad exploration.

Pros & Cons
Pros: Budget-friendly choice, decreases reliance on car rentals, convenient for connecting to main towns.
Cons: Limited timetables and routes, may not be ideal for reaching all villages, longer journey times compared to automobiles.

Tip: Purchase a multi-day bus pass if you plan on utilizing public transport regularly for financial savings.

Lace Up Your Boots: Exploring the Cotswolds on Foot

The Cotswolds are a walker's delight. Numerous pathways weave across undulating hills, past picturesque villages, and along idyllic waterways.

Highlights: Immerse yourself in the splendor of the Cotswolds at your own leisure. Hiking allows you to discover hidden jewels, lovely communities, and breathtaking overlooks unreachable by car.

Walking Trails: The Cotswolds Way National Trail, a 102-mile trail, is the crown jewel. Numerous shorter routes cater to all levels, from peaceful family-friendly strolls to strenuous hill climbs.

Pricing: Walking is free! Though some vehicle parks near trailheads may have costs (usually roughly £2-£5 per day).

Pros & Cons
Pros: Immersive experience, healthy and eco-friendly way to explore, uncover hidden treasures unreachable by car.
Cons: Limited range compared to car, requires strong planning and navigation skills, weather dependent (be prepared for all circumstances).

Planning Your Hike: Research trials that meet your fitness level and interests. Pack comfortable walking shoes, weather-appropriate clothing, and lots of water. Consider getting a Cotswolds walking map for route direction.

Renting a Car: Freedom to Roam at Your Own Pace

For ultimate flexibility and the chance to explore every nook and cranny of the Cotswolds, consider renting a car.

Highlights: Explore the Cotswolds on your own terms, stop at lovely villages on a whim, design a personalized route that meets your interests, enjoy the gorgeous drives through authentically English countryside.

Prices: Rental car fees vary depending on the automobile type, rental provider, and season. Budget roughly £30-£80 every day, not counting petrol expenditures. Factor in the cost of automobile parking, which might vary based on location (usually roughly £1-£5 per hour in town centers).

Pros & Cons

Pros: Freedom and flexibility to explore at your own pace, reach hidden villages inaccessible by public transport, convenient for day trips to surrounding areas like Oxford or Bath.

Cons: Requires good navigation skills, parking can be limited in some villages, traffic congestion can occur during peak seasons (especially around popular attractions).

Planning Your Road Trip: Plan your route using Google Maps or the Automobile Association (AA) route planner: www.theaa.com/route-planner. Consider getting a Cotswolds road map for precise guidance, especially for beautiful byways.

Driving in the UK: Remember, Brits drive on the left-hand side of the road. Ensure you have the right driver's license and educate yourself with traffic restrictions before hitting the road.

Cycling Adventures: Pedal Through Picturesque Landscapes

The Cotswolds' moderate hills and picturesque byways are great for exploring by bicycle. Several firms provide bike rentals, allowing you to discover the countryside at a leisurely pace.

Highlights: Enjoy the fresh air and magnificent views as you pedal between communities. Discover hidden jewels along peaceful country paths unreachable by motor.

Pricing: Bicycle rental fees vary depending on the type of bike and rental time. Expect to pay roughly £20-£40 per day for a typical bike.

Pros & Cons
Pros: Eco-friendly way to wander around, healthy and active way to travel, enjoy the scenic beauty of the Cotswolds from a distinct perspective, discover hidden gems inaccessible by car.
Cons: Weather dependent (be prepared for all conditions), may require a good level of fitness for hillier sections, limited luggage capacity compared to cars.

Planning Your Cycle Trip: Research bike rental providers in Cotswolds towns like Cirencester or Bourton-on-the-Water. Choose a path that meets your fitness level and interests. Invest in a good quality helmet and ensure your bike is in good operating order before starting off.

Note: Cycle carefully, observe local traffic restrictions, and be mindful of pedestrians, especially on narrow country lanes.

Choosing Your Perfect Mode of Transport:

The Cotswolds offer a range of ways to explore, each with its own merits. Consider your budget, interests, and travel style while making your decision. From budget-friendly public transit to the flexibility of a vehicle rental, or the invigorating pleasure of exploring on foot or by bike, there's a perfect method for you to discover the enchantment of the Cotswolds.

So tie up your walking boots, rent a bike, or buckle up for a picturesque drive. The Cotswolds await, eager to unfold their timeless beauty at your own leisure.

CHAPTER 4:

WHERE TO STAY

Discovering the stunning beauty of the Cotswolds begins with finding the best place to stay. From magnificent spa complexes situated amidst huge rural estates to modest cottages in beautiful villages, the Cotswolds provides a broad choice of accommodation alternatives to meet every traveler's preferences. Whether you're seeking a pleasant Luxury Retreat experience or an exciting camping trip under the stars, the Cotswolds delivers wonderful stays amidst its stunning scenery.

Luxurious Retreats: Spa Resort and Country Estate

Indulge in unrivaled splendor amidst the rolling hills of the Cotswolds. From stately spa resorts to grand country estates, discover opulent luxuries and superb service in this exquisite English countryside location.

Spa Resorts: The Lygon Arms

Indulge in luxury and relaxation at The Lygon Arms, a historic spa resort set in the heart of Broadway village.

Highlights: Elegant spa facilities, award-winning dining, magnificent accommodations.
Activities: Spa treatments, scenic hikes, great dining experiences.
Pricing: Rooms start at £250 per night.
Check-in/out: Check-in: 3:00 PM, Check-out: 11:00 AM.
Address: High St, Broadway WR12 7DU, United Kingdom.

How to Get There: Located in the village of Broadway, easily accessible by vehicle from large cities like London and Birmingham. Alternatively, the nearest train station is Evesham, roughly 6 miles away.
Closest Must-See Sites: Broadway Tower, Hidcote Manor Garden.
Website: www.lygonarmshotel.co.uk

Country Estates: Ellenborough Park

Experience grandeur and elegance at Ellenborough Park, a beautiful country estate situated on the outskirts of Cheltenham.

Highlights: Historic architecture, spacious grounds, Michelin-starred food.

Activities: Horse riding, falconry adventures, afternoon tea.
Pricing: Rooms start at £350 per night.
Check-in/out: Check-in: 3:00 PM, Check-out: 11:00 AM.
Address: Southam Rd, Cheltenham GL52 3NJ, United Kingdom.

How to Get There: Located near Cheltenham, roughly 2 hours from London by vehicle. The nearest train station is Cheltenham Spa, about a 15-minute drive away.
Closest Must-See Sites: Sudeley Castle, Cotswold Farm Park.
Website: www.ellenboroughpark.com

Quaint Villages: Charming Cottages and Holiday Rentals

Step back in time as you meander through the lovely alleyways of the Cotswolds' small villages. Admire beautiful stone cottages, lovely tearooms, and busy market squares, all steeped in timeless English charm.

Charming Cottages: StayCotswold

Immerse yourself in the beauty of the Cotswolds with StayCotswold's collection of quaint and warm cottages dotted around the region.

Highlights: Traditional Cotswold building, lovely settings, fully-equipped kitchens.

Activities: Exploring village pubs, picturesque walks, visiting local markets.
Pricing: Prices vary based on cottage size and location, beginning at £150 per night.
Check-in/out: Check-in: 4:00 PM, Check-out: 10:00 AM.
Address: Multiple places in the Cotswolds.

How to Get There: Directions supplied following booking confirmation. Easily accessible by automobile from large cities or via public transport to adjacent communities.
Closest Must-See Sites: Bourton-on-the-Water, Bibury.
Website: www.staycotswold.com

Holiday Rentals: Character Cottages

Discover your own slice of Cotswold heaven with Character Cottages, offering a selection of holiday homes in lovely village locations.

Highlights: Cozy decor, historic details, pet-friendly options.
Activities: Visiting historic landmarks, countryside picnics, visiting local shops.
Pricing: Prices vary depending on house size and location, starting at £120 per night.
Check-in/out: Check-in: 3:00 PM, Check-out: 10:00 AM.
Address: Multiple places in the Cotswolds.

How to Get There: Directions supplied following booking confirmation. Easily accessible via automobile or public transit to adjacent towns.
Closest Must-See Sites: Stow-on-the-Wold, The Slaughters.
Website: www.character-cottages.co.uk

Camping Under the Stars: Campsites and Glamping Options

Escape the hustle and bustle and reconnect with nature in the Cotswolds. Set up camp under a blanket of stars, surrounded by the tranquil beauty of lush landscapes and serenaded by the sounds of the countryside.

Campsites: Cotswold Farm Park Camping

Embrace the great outdoors at Cotswold Farm Park Camping, offering a rustic camping experience on a working farm.

Highlights: Tranquil surroundings, farm activities, on-site conveniences.
Activities: Animal feeding, nature walks, campfire cooking.
Pricing: Tent pitches start at £20 per night.
Check-in/out: Check-in: 2:00 PM, Check-out: 11:00 AM.
Address: Guiting Power, Cheltenham GL54 5FL, United Kingdom.

How to Get There: Located near Cheltenham, roughly 2 hours from London by vehicle. The nearest train station is Moreton-in-Marsh, about a 15-minute drive away.
Closest Must-See Sites: Broadway Tower, Cotswold Wildlife Park.
Website: www.cotswoldfarmpark.co.uk/camping

Glamping Options: Abbey Home Farm

Experience the beauty of nature with a touch of luxury at Abbey Home Farm's glamping site, hidden amidst organic agriculture.

45

Highlights: Eco-friendly accomodation, agricultural tours, farm shop.
Activities: Yoga classes, organic farm activities, stargazing.
Pricing: Glamping pods start at £100 per night.
Check-in/out: Check-in: 3:00 PM, Check-out: 11:00 AM.
Address: Burford Rd, Cirencester GL7 5HF, United Kingdom.

How to Get There: Located near Cirencester, roughly 1.5 hours from London by vehicle. The nearest train station is Kemble, about a 20-minute drive away.
Closest Must-See Sites: Cirencester Amphitheatre, Cotswold Water Park.
Website:
www.theorganicfarmshop.co.uk/accommodation/glamping

Whether you're looking for a posh hideaway, a lovely hamlet experience, or a rustic camping excursion, the Cotswolds provides a variety of lodging alternatives to suit your preferences. From sophisticated spa resorts to modest cottages and camping beneath the stars, get soaked in the beauty and calm of this lovely region.

CHAPTER 5:

EXPLORING COTSWOLDS

Iconic Villages and Towns: Must-Visit Destinations

Exploring the Cotswolds' historic villages and towns is a pleasant experience, offering a look into pure English charm. Here are several must-visit sites, along with updated information on reaching them, cost, and recommended tour operators:

1. Bourton-on-the-Water: Known as the "Venice of the Cotswolds" for its picturesque bridges over the River Windrush, Bourton-on-the-Water is a must-visit. To access it, you can take a train to the nearby town of Moreton-in-Marsh and then catch a bus or taxi to Bourton. Alternatively, driving is convenient, with abundant parking available.

Pricing: Entry to most sites in Bourton is free, however some may require a nominal fee.

Recommended Tour Operator:
-Cotswolds Guided Tours:

www.cotswoldsguidedtours.co.uk offers educational and personalized tours of Bourton-on-the-Water and neighboring locations.

2. Stow-on-the-Wold: This medieval market town features attractive alleys lined with honey-colored buildings and is famed for its antique shops. Stow-on-the-Wold is accessible by train to Moreton-in-Marsh, followed by a short bus or cab ride.

Pricing: Prices vary for activities such as shopping, dining, and visiting sites.

Recommended Tour Operator:
Go Cotswolds www.gocotswolds.co.uk offers guided excursions of Stow-on-the-Wold and other Cotswold sites, providing insight into the town's history and culture.

3. Broadway: Often referred to as the "Jewel of the Cotswolds," Broadway is known for its large high street dotted with independent shops, galleries, and cafés. The nearest train station is Evesham, from where you may take a bus or taxi to Broadway.

Pricing: Free to roam the streets, however charges may apply for specific sights and activities.

Recommended Tour Operator:
Cotswold Walks www.cotswoldwalks.com offers guided walking tours of Broadway and the surrounding countryside, allowing tourists to enjoy the area's natural beauty and legacy.

4. Chipping Campden: This quaint market town is famed for its magnificent terraced buildings and its wool trade heritage. It's accessible by train to Moreton-in-Marsh, followed by a short bus or taxi travel.

Pricing: Entry to most sites in Chipping Campden is free, but there may be costs for specialized activities.

Recommended Trip Operator: Cotswold Exploring www.cotswoldexploring.co.uk offers bespoke tours of Chipping Campden, providing insights into its architecture, history, and local culture.

When planning your journey to the Cotswolds, it's recommended to check the current travel information and any COVID-19 recommendations or restrictions. Additionally, reserving excursions in advance is encouraged to secure your position and ensure a seamless and enjoyable experience.

Historic Landmarks: Castles, Manors, and Abbeys

Exploring the historic landmarks of the Cotswolds, including castles, manors, and abbeys, offers a fascinating view into the region's rich legacy. Here are some important places, along with updated information on reaching them, pricing, and related tour operators:

1. Sudeley Castle: With over 1,000 years of history, Sudeley Castle is one of the Cotswolds' most renowned sights. Situated near Winchcombe, it's accessible by vehicle or public transit. The nearest train station is Cheltenham Spa, from where you may take a cab or bus to the castle.

Pricing: Admission charges vary based on the time of year and any special events. Discounts are often given for seniors, kids, and families.

Recommended tour operator: Cotswold Journeys (www.cotswoldjourneys.com) offers guided excursions that include trips to Sudeley Castle, providing insights into its history and significance.

2. Blenheim Palace: Located in adjacent Oxfordshire, Blenheim Palace is a UNESCO World Heritage Site and the birthplace of Sir Winston Churchill. It's easily accessible by vehicle or train. The nearest train station is Oxford, and from there, you may take a bus or taxi to the palace.

Pricing: Admission charges vary depending on the type of ticket and any special exhibitions or activities. Discounts are often available for online bookings and groups.

Recommended Tour Operator: Premium Tours (www.premiumtours.co.uk) conducts day trips from London to Blenheim Palace, including guided tours of the palace and its large grounds.

3. Hailes Abbey: This historic Cistercian abbey in Winchcombe is a calm and atmospheric site to explore. To access it, you can drive or take public transport to Winchcombe, followed by a short cab ride or lovely walk to the abbey.

Pricing: Admission to Hailes Abbey is normally free for English Heritage members, with a nominal cost for non-members. Donations are appreciated to help the site's upkeep.

Recommended Tour Operator: Cotswolds Adventures (www.cotswoldsadventures.co.uk) offers guided walking excursions that include trips to Hailes Abbey, allowing tourists to learn about its history and significance.

4. Snowshill Manor: This National Trust house near Broadway is famed for its varied collection of art, crafts, and antiques, acquired by its former owner, Charles Paget Wade. It's accessible by automobile or public transit, with the nearest train station at Moreton-in-Marsh.

Pricing: Admission charges vary depending on membership status and any special exhibitions. Discounts are often available for National Trust members and families.

Recommended Tour Operator: The Cotswold Tour Company (www.cotswoldtourcompany.com) offers bespoke trips that can include visits to Snowshill Manor, providing insights into its intriguing collections and the life of Charles Paget Wade.

When arranging your visit to these historic landmarks, it's recommended to check the latest operating hours, entrance charges, and any COVID-19 requirements or restrictions. Booking tickets in advance is suggested, especially during peak tourist seasons, to ensure availability and avoid disappointment.

Natural Wonders: Gardens, Parks, and Nature Reserves

Exploring the Cotswolds offers a pleasant immersion into its natural beauties, including gardens, parks, and nature reserves.

1. Hidcote Manor Garden: Renowned for its elaborate outdoor "rooms" and bright plant collections, Hidcote Manor Garden offers a lovely hideaway for nature enthusiasts and garden lovers. Located near Chipping Campden, Gloucestershire, it's easily accessible by vehicle or public transit.

2. Cotswold Wildlife Park and Gardens: Home to a vast collection of exotic animals and gorgeous landscaped gardens, this park in Burford provides an enriching experience for visitors of all ages. You may reach it by vehicle or train, with abundant parking accessible onsite.

3. Blenheim Palace: While technically not in the Cotswolds, Blenheim Palace's enormous grounds and formal gardens make it a must-visit site nearby. Situated in Woodstock, Oxfordshire, it's accessible by vehicle or public transportation, including buses and trains.

4. Cotswold Water Park: Spanning over 40 square miles, this network of lakes and wildlife reserves offers numerous chances for outdoor excursions, from birdwatching to water sports. Various entry locations enable simple access by car or bicycle.

How to Get There:
- By Car: The Cotswolds is well-connected by road networks, making it accessible for travelers to explore at their own pace. Major routes include the M5, M40, and A40.
- By Train: Several towns in the Cotswolds, such as Cheltenham, Stroud, and Moreton-in-Marsh, have train stations operated by Great Western train and other operators.
- By Bus: Local bus routes link many Cotswold villages and towns, giving an economical and eco-friendly form of transit.

Pricing & Relevant Tour Operators Websites:
-**Hidcote Manor Garden**: Entry costs vary based on the time of year and special events. For updated price and booking information, see the National Trust website: www.nationaltrust.org.uk/hidcote

- **Cotswold Wildlife Park and Gardens**: Ticket rates and opening hours can be found on the official website: www.cotswoldwildlifepark.co.uk

-**Blenheim Palace**: Explore ticket options and organize your visit via the official website: www.blenheimpalace.com

- **Cotswold Water Park**: Admission to most portions of the water park is free, although particular activities may have associated expenses. Check the Cotswold Water Park Trust website for more details:
www.waterpark.org

Additionally, for guided excursions and specialized experiences in the Cotswolds, consider reputed tour providers such as:
-**Cotswolds Guided Tours**: Offering bespoke guided tours according to your interests and preferences:
https://cotswoldsguidedtours.co.uk
- **Cotswolds Adventures**: Providing guided tours, outdoor activities, and cultural experiences in the Cotswolds region: www.cotswoldsadventures.co.uk

Exploring the Cotswolds promises an amazing tour through its natural beauty and cultural heritage, with options to fit every traveler's preferences and budget.

Culinary Delights: Food and Drink Experiences in Cotswolds

Exploring the gastronomic wonders of the Cotswolds is a treat for food and drink connoisseurs, with a variety of experiences to indulge in.

1. Daylesford Organic Farm: Nestled in Kingham, Daylesford Organic Farm offers a farm-to-table experience with organic products, cooking workshops, and farm tours. Easily accessible by vehicle or train to Kingham station, followed by a short cab trip. Prices vary for excursions and classes.

-**Website**: www.daylesford.com

2. Cotswolds Distillery: Located in Stourton, the Cotswolds Distillery offers guided tours where visitors can learn about gin and whiskey manufacturing and enjoy samples. Accessible by automobile or train to local stations, followed by a short cab journey. Tour rates vary.

- **Website**: www.cotswoldsdistillery.com

3. Local Food and Drink Tours: Various guided culinary tours are available, giving visits to local producers, artisanal food outlets, and traditional pubs. These trips offer the best of Cotswold cuisine and beverages. Accessible by automobile or public transit, depending on the trip route. Tour rates vary.

When planning your gastronomic excursion in the Cotswolds, consider checking for any seasonal events or festivals honoring local food and drink. Booking in advance for tours and classes is advisable to reserve your position, especially during peak tourist seasons.

CHAPTER 6:

EXPERIENCING COTSWOLDS CULTURE

Festivals and Events: Celebrating Local Traditions

Festivals:

1. Cheltenham Jazz Festival
- When: Late April/Early May 2024 (Exact dates vary)
- Where: Cheltenham
- Details: Enjoy world-class jazz performances in several venues in Cheltenham, featuring both known musicians and emerging talents. Pricing: Ticket costs vary depending on the event and seats, ranging from £10 to £50 per ticket.

2. Lechlade Music Festival
   - When: May 2024 (Exact dates vary)
   - Where: Lechlade-on-Thames
   - Details: Experience a family-friendly music festival including a broad roster of live musicians, food vendors, and entertainment for all ages. Pricing: Weekend tickets

normally vary from £50 to £100 per adult, with reductions for children and families.

3. Cheltenham Food and Drink Festival
 - When: June 2024 (Exact dates change)
   - Where: Cheltenham
   - Details: Sample amazing local produce, artisanal cuisine, and beverages while enjoying cooking demos, tastings, and live entertainment. Pricing: Entry to the festival is normally free, however some activities and tastings may require purchase of tokens or tickets.

4. Tetbury Woolsack Races
   - When: May 2025 (Exact dates vary)
   - Where: Tetbury
   - Details: Witness the unusual tradition of locals running up and down the steep streets of Tetbury carrying heavy woolsacks, followed by a bright street celebration. Pricing: Free to attend the races, with optional expenditures for food, drinks, and souvenirs at the festival.

5. Cirencester Summer Sausage and Ale Festival
   - When: July 2025 (Exact dates vary)
   - Where: Cirencester
   - Details: Indulge in a range of sausages and ales from local producers, complemented by live music and entertainment in the old market town of Cirencester.

Pricing: Entry to the festival is normally free, with costs for food, beverages, and specific activities.

6. Stroud Fringe Festival
   - When: August 2025 (Exact dates vary)
   - Where: Stroud
- Details: Immerse yourself in a celebration of music, arts, and culture at this colorful neighborhood festival with live music, street performances, and art installations. Pricing: Most activities at the festival are free, with donations suggested for some performances.

7. Moreton Show
   - When: September 2025 (Exact dates vary)
   - Where: Moreton-in-Marsh
   - Details: Experience one of the largest agricultural exhibitions in the Cotswolds, with livestock contests, equestrian events, food vendors, and family entertainment. Pricing: Tickets normally vary from £10 to £20 per adult, with discounts for children and families.

8. Broadway Arts Festival
   - When: June 2025 (Exact dates vary)
   - Where: Broadway
   - Details: Celebrate the arts in the lovely village of Broadway with exhibitions, workshops, performances, and discussions featuring local artists and artisans.

Pricing: Entry to some events may be free, while others may require ticket purchases ranging from £5 to £20.

9. Tetbury Music Festival
   - When: October 2025 (Exact dates vary)
   - Where: Tetbury
   - Details: Enjoy classical music concerts given by renowned performers in the historic setting of Tetbury's churches and venues. Pricing: Ticket costs vary depending on the event and seats, ranging from £15 to £50 per ticket.

10. Chipping Campden Literature Festival
    - When: May 2025 (Exact dates vary)
    - Where: Chipping Campden
    - Details: Engage with authors, poets, and speakers from around the world at this literary festival, offering talks, readings, and book signings in the picturesque town of Chipping Campden. Pricing: Ticket costs vary based on the event, with some free events and others ranging from £10 to £30 per ticket.

Events:

1. May Day Celebrations
   - When: May 1, 2024 - Where: Various villages in the Cotswolds

- Details: Experience traditional May Day activities including maypole dance, morris dancing, and village fairs in towns and villages around the Cotswolds. Pricing: Free to attend, with optional expenditures for food, drinks, and souvenirs.

2. Cotswold Show and Food Festival
   - When: July 5-6, 2024
- Where: Cirencester Park
- Details: Attend one of the region's largest agricultural exhibitions featuring cattle presentations, equestrian activities, food stalls, craft demonstrations, and family entertainment. Pricing: Tickets normally vary from £10 to £20 per adult, with discounts for children and families.

3. Gloucester Tall Ships Festival
   - When: August 23-26, 2024
- Where: Gloucester Docks
   - Details: Witness spectacular tall ships docking at Gloucester Docks, surrounded by maritime-themed activities, live music, street entertainment, and fireworks. Pricing: Free to attend, with costs for certain activities and trips.

4. Bourton-on-the-Water Football in the River
 - When: August Bank Holiday (date varies)
 - Where: Bourton-on-the-Water

- Details: Watch as teams battle in a unique football match played in the river, followed by a fun-filled day of festivities and entertainment for fans. Pricing: Free to attend, with optional donations for charity and purchases for food, drinks, and souvenirs.

5. Cheltenham Literature Festival
   - When: October 4-13, 2024
   - Where: Cheltenham
   - Details: Engage with authors, poets, and speakers from around the world at one of the oldest and most prominent literary festivals in the UK. Pricing: Ticket costs vary based on the event, ranging from £10 to £30 per ticket.

6. Blenheim Palace Christmas Market
   - When: November 21-December 15, 2024 - Where: Blenheim Palace
   - Details: Experience the enchantment of Christmas at Blenheim Palace's seasonal market, featuring over 100 stalls providing presents, decorations, food, and drink. Pricing: Free access to the market, with costs for parking and optional items.

7. Cirencester Advent Festival
   - When: December 1, 2024
- Where: Cirencester - Details: Join in the festivities as Cirencester comes alive with Christmas lights, live

music, street entertainment, and a traditional Advent procession. Pricing: Free to visit, with charges for certain activities and items.

8. New Year's Eve Fireworks in Tewkesbury
   - When: December 31, 2024 - Where: Tewkesbury
   - Details: Ring in the New Year with a stunning fireworks show over Tewkesbury Abbey, followed by parties and live music in the town center. Pricing: Free to witness the fireworks display, with payments for some events and food and drink purchases during the celebrations.

9. Cotswold Way Challenge
- When: May 2025 (Exact dates vary)
- Where: Cotswold Way (Starts in Bath)
- Details: Take on the challenge of walking, jogging, or running the scenic Cotswold Way trail, covering distances ranging from 25 km to 100km over one or two days. Pricing: Entry fees range from £30 to £100 per participant, depending on the selected distance and category.

10. Cotswold Hare Trail
- When: Throughout 2025 (Exact dates vary)
- Where: Various locations across the Cotswolds
- Details: Follow the Cotswold Hare Trail, an art trail featuring beautifully decorated hare sculptures displayed

in towns and villages throughout the region, showcasing local artists' talents. Pricing: Free to follow the trail, with optional donations encouraged to support local charities and art organizations.

Art and Craft Galleries: Showcasing Creative Talents

Exploring the cultural core of the Cotswolds through its art and craft galleries is an enriching experience. Lets navigate like a local with the following:

1. New Brewery Arts - Cirencester: Situated in Cirencester's heart, this contemporary craft center shows varied artworks by local and national talents. Visitors can delve into exhibitions exhibiting ceramics, textiles, and glassware. Workshops and classes are provided for anyone willing to better their creative skills.
- Pricing: Admission is normally free, with workshop prices fluctuating.
-Transportation: Cirencester is accessible by vehicle and bus, with adjacent parking. The Kemble train station is roughly 6 kilometers away.
-Website: www.newbreweryarts.org.uk

2. Gallery Pangolin - Chalford: Specializing in modern and contemporary sculpture, Gallery Pangolin showcases works by prominent artists including Lynn Chadwick and Elisabeth Frink. Enjoy free entrance amidst the gorgeous Cotswold countryside.

-Transportation: Best accessed by automobile, with limited parking close.

3. Court Barn Museum - Chipping Campden: Housed in a historic structure, Court Barn Museum showcases the Arts & Crafts movement's craftsmanship. Explore furniture, metalwork, and textiles by prominent designers like C.R. Ashbee and Gordon Russell.

- Pricing: Admission costs normally range from £5 to £8 for adults.

- Transportation: Accessible by vehicle and bus, with limited parking close.

-Website: https://courtbarn.org.uk

4. The Wilson - Cheltenham Art Gallery & Museum: Offering a broad collection of art and antiques, The Wilson in Cheltenham contains current and historical displays, including an excellent Arts and Crafts collection.

-Pricing: Free entrance, donations welcome.

-Transportation: Easily accessible by train, bus, and vehicle, located in the town center.

-Website: www.cheltenhammuseum.org.uk

5. Stratford-upon-Avon Art Gallery: Just outside the Cotswolds, this gallery shows modern paintings, sculptures, and ceramics by emerging and recognized artists.
- **Transportation**: Accessible by train, bus, and vehicle, with parking accessible in the town center.

6. Victoria Art Gallery - Bath: Bath's Victoria Art Gallery showcases a range of temporary exhibitions, featuring a mix of local and national artistic skills.
- **Transportation**: Accessible by train, bus, and vehicle, located in the city core.
-Website: www.victoriagal.org.uk

7. Broadway Museum and Art Gallery: In the lovely village of Broadway, this museum and gallery display the region's rich history and current art.
- Pricing: Admission rates range from £4 to £8 for adults.
-Transportation: Accessible by vehicle and bus, with parking available in the village.
-Website: https://broadwaymuseum.org.uk

Museums and Heritage Sites: Delving into Cotswolds' Rich History

Let's plunge into the intriguing culture of the Cotswolds with its museums and heritage sites.

1. The Mechanical Music Museum - Northleach: Immerse yourself in captivating tunes and sophisticated engineering with an astounding selection of mechanical musical instruments. Visitors can gaze at music boxes, player pianos, and orchestras, and even try operating some instruments. Admission prices apply, with reductions possible. Located in Northleach, accessible by automobile or public transportation.
Website: www.mechanicalmusic.co.uk

2. Snowshill Manor and Garden - Snowshill: Delve into the varied world of eccentric collector Charles Paget Wade at Snowshill Manor. Explore rooms filled with different things, from Japanese armor to English antiquities, and promenade through well managed gardens. Admission costs apply, with savings for National Trust members. Snowshill is best reached by driving.
Website: www.nationaltrust.org.uk/snowshill-manor-and-garden

3. The Corinium Museum - Cirencester: Uncover the Roman past of Cirencester at this award-winning museum. Explore immersive displays and artifacts showing life in Roman Britain. Admission prices apply, with reductions possible. Located in Cirencester, accessible by car or public transportation.
Website: https://coriniummuseum.org

4. The Painswick Rococo Garden - Painswick: Step into a fantastical world of 18th-century pleasure gardens showcasing magnificent follies and scenic views. Wander around beautiful grounds and seasonal exhibits. Admission prices apply, with reductions possible. Painswick is best reached by automobile.
Website: https://www.rococogarden.org.uk

5. Stanway House and Fountain - Stanway: Explore the grandeur of Stanway House, a spectacular Jacobean palace with the world's tallest gravity-fed fountain. Guided tours offer insights into its past. Admission costs apply. Stanway is best reached by automobile.
Website: www.stanwayfountain.co.uk

6. Hailes Abbey - Winchcombe: Journey back in time to a medieval Cistercian abbey. Explore eerie ruins and learn about the abbey's history. Admission prices apply, with reductions possible. Winchcombe is accessible by automobile or public transportation.

Website:
www.english-heritage.org.uk/visit/places/hailes-abbey

7. The Cotswold motorsport Museum - Bourton-on-the-Water: Discover the evolution of transportation in a lovely museum dedicated to motorsport history. View classic automobiles, motorcycles, and bicycles, and explore interactive displays. Admission prices apply, with reductions possible. Located in Bourton-on-the-Water, accessible by car or bus.
Website: www.cotswoldmotoringmuseum.co.uk

Engaging with Locals: Workshops, Classes, and Cultural Exchanges

Let's bathe in Cotswolds culture by engaging with locals through seminars, classes, and cultural exchanges.

1. Craft Workshops at New Brewery Arts - Cirencester: Participate in hands-on craft programs ranging from pottery and ceramics to weaving and jewelry creation. Learn directly from local artists and gain insight into traditional Cotswolds crafts.
-Website: www.newbreweryarts.org.uk

- Transportation: Easily accessible by car and bus. Cirencester may also be accessible by train from major cities.

2. Cooking workshops in Cotswolds Cuisine: Discover the flavors of Cotswolds cuisine by taking cooking workshops conducted by local chefs. Learn to cook traditional dishes utilizing fresh, locally-sourced ingredients, and get an appreciation of the region's culinary past.
- Availability: Look for classes given by local cooking schools or restaurants in locations like Cheltenham, Stow-on-the-Wold, or Broadway.
- Transportation: Most towns in the Cotswolds are easily accessible by car, bus, or train.

3. Walking Tours with Local Guides: Join guided walking tours conducted by knowledgeable locals who can share stories and insights about the Cotswolds' history, architecture, and culture. Explore picturesque villages, historic landmarks, and hidden gems off the usual route.
- Availability: Look for tour companies or local guides conducting themed walks, such as literary tours in Chipping Campden or ghost walks in Burford.
- Transportation: Tours often start from town centers and may require walking or short driving to neighboring sights.

4. Language and Cultural Exchange Programs: Connect with locals through language and cultural exchange programs, where you may meet residents, practice English, and learn about Cotswolds traditions firsthand. Look for community centers, libraries, or internet platforms offering exchange opportunities.
- Availability: Check with local community organizations or internet platforms specializing in cultural exchanges.
- Transportation: Programs may take place in numerous locations throughout the Cotswolds, so consider transportation choices dependent on the exact program location.

5. Art and Photography Workshops: Hone your artistic skills and capture the beauty of the Cotswolds scenery with art and photography workshops offered by local artists and photographers. Learn new methods while experiencing stunning scenery and village sights.
- Availability: Look for classes provided by galleries, art centers, or independent artists in towns like Cheltenham, Stroud, or Tetbury.
- Transportation: Depending on the workshop location, transportation choices may include vehicle, bus, or train.

CHAPTER 7:

INSIDER TIPS & LOCAL SECRETS

Off-the-Beaten-Path Spots: Secret Spots Revealed

1. Woodchester Mansion:
-Location: Near Stroud
-Description: Explore the creepy yet magnificent Woodchester Mansion, an incomplete Gothic revival mansion surrounded by serene countryside. This hidden jewel provides guided excursions exposing its fascinating history and architectural delights.
-Insider Tip: Check the schedule for special events like ghost tours and paranormal investigations for a truly unique experience.

-How to Get There: Woodchester Mansion is accessible by automobile from Stroud. Parking is provided onsite. Alternatively, you can take a taxi or ride-sharing service from Stroud.
Website: www.woodchestermansion.org.uk

2. The Rollright Stones:
-Location: Near Chipping Norton

-Description: Delve into ancient history at The Rollright Stones, a prehistoric stone circle steeped in myth and tradition. Situated amidst the lovely Cotswold countryside, this lesser-known place offers a tranquil atmosphere for contemplation and discovery.
-Insider Tip: Visit during sunset or sunrise for stunning vistas and a beautiful mood.

-How to Get There: The Rollright Stones are best reached by automobile. There is minimal parking accessible near the venue. Alternatively, you can take a taxi or local bus to Chipping Norton and then walk or cycle to the stones.
Website: www.rollrightstones.co.uk

3. Snowshill Manor and Garden:
-Location: Near Broadway
-Description: Step inside the diverse world of Snowshill Manor, a National Trust property filled with the quirky collections of its former owner, Charles Paget Wade. From Japanese armor to musical instruments, each chamber is a treasure trove of rarities.
-Insider Tip: Arrive early to avoid crowds and take advantage of the calm environment in the gorgeous hillside garden.

-How to Get There: Snowshill Manor is accessible by automobile from Broadway. Limited parking is offered

onsite for visitors. Additionally, several local tour operators provide guided tours to Snowshill Manor from adjacent towns.
-Website: www.nationaltrust.org.uk/snowshill-manor-and-garden

4. The Secret Cottage Tour:
-Location: Various villages in the Cotswolds
-Description: Embark on a totally immersive experience with The Secret Cottage Tour, a guided excursion through hidden towns, secret gardens, and beautiful tea houses. Get intimate knowledge from a local guide while eating homemade goodies and magnificent scenery.
-Insider Tip: Book in advance, as excursions are limited to small groups and tend to fill up quickly.

-How to Get There: The meeting point for The Secret Cottage Tour varies depending on the tour route. Detailed instructions will be supplied upon booking. Most trips start from popular Cotswold towns like Moreton-in-Marsh or Chipping Campden.
Website: https://www.secretcottage.co.uk

5. Hailes Abbey:
-Location: Near Winchcombe
-Description: Discover the remains of Hailes Abbey, a medieval Cistercian abbey set in the Cotswold countryside. Explore the evocative ruins and learn about

its history as a destination of pilgrimage and royal patronage.

-Insider Tip: Combine your visit with a walk along the neighboring Cotswold Way for panoramic views of the surrounding environment.

-How to Get There: Hailes Abbey is accessible by automobile from Winchcombe. Limited parking is offered onsite for visitors. Alternatively, you can take a taxi or hike from Winchcombe along the Cotswold Way. Website: www.english-heritage.org.uk/visit/places/hailes-abbey

Practical Advice from Locals & Expats

1. Explore Beyond the Main Villages:

Tip: While prominent villages like Bourton-on-the-Water and Stow-on-the-Wold are must-visit places, don't skip out on discovering the smaller, less crowded villages that provide equally charming experiences. Places like Naunton, Stanton, and Upper Slaughter are hidden jewels waiting to be discovered.

2. Timing is Key:

Tip: Visit major locations early in the morning or late in the afternoon to avoid the crowds. Many tourists like to arrive around lunchtime, so plan your visits appropriately for a more enjoyable experience. Additionally, try going during the off-peak season (late fall or winter) for a quieter and more intimate setting.

3. Get Lost in Nature:

Tip: Take use of the Cotswolds' enormous network of footpaths and bridleways to explore the lovely landscape. Whether you're an ardent hiker or prefer a leisurely stroll, there are paths ideal for all levels. Be sure to pack a picnic and soak in the gorgeous vistas along the route.

4. Embrace Local Cuisine:

Tip: Don't leave the Cotswolds without sampling some of the region's culinary delights. From classic pub meals to gourmet dining experiences, there's something for every pallet. Be sure to try local favorites like Cotswold lamb, Gloucestershire cheese, and scrumpy cider for a true experience of the region.

5. Engage with the Community:

Tip: Take the opportunity to chat with residents and expats who call the Cotswolds home. They can offer vital insider information, recommendations, and hidden jewels that you won't discover in guidebooks. Whether it's striking up a conversation at a local bar or attending a community event, mingling with residents adds richness to your Cotswolds experience.

6. Plan for Variable Weather:

Tip: The weather in the Cotswolds can be unpredictable, so it's necessary to come prepared. Pack layers, waterproof gear, and sturdy walking shoes, especially if you plan to visit the countryside. Always check the weather forecast before venturing out and be flexible with your agenda to make the most of sunny days and adapt to inclement weather.

7. Respect the Environment:

Tip: Help maintain the natural beauty of the Cotswolds by practicing responsible tourism. Respect wildlife habitats, follow designated routes, and dispose of rubbish correctly. Consider carrying a reusable water bottle and shopping bag to minimize your environmental effect during your visit.

By following this practical advice from locals and expatriates, you'll have a pleasant and satisfying experience touring the Cotswolds while gaining insight into the region's culture, cuisine, and natural beauty.

CHAPTER 8:

OUTDOOR ADVENTURES

Rambling Routes: Scenic Walks and Hikes

Outdoor excursions in the Cotswolds provide stunning walks and hikes for first-time travelers. Here's everything you need to know:

1. Cotswold Way: Choose day walks or multi-day expeditions. Prices vary for motels along the route. Accessible by train to several starting places.
-Highlights: Stunning countryside views, medieval villages, and old sites.
-Website: www.nationaltrail.co.uk/en_GB/trails/cotswold-way

2. Bibury and Arlington Row: Free to explore. Accessible by vehicle or bus from adjacent towns.
-Highlights: Iconic Arlington Row cottages, lovely riverbank walks, and typical village charm.
-Website: www.bibury.com

3. Broadway Tower: Entry fee for tower access. Accessible by automobile or public footpaths.

-Highlights: Panoramic views from the tower, picturesque walking routes, and wildlife spotting chances.
-Website: https://broadwaytower.co.uk

4. The Slaughters: Free to explore. Accessible by automobile or beautiful treks from adjacent villages.
-Highlights: Picturesque stone houses, calm riverbank walkways, and old bridges.
-Website:
Upper Slaughter (www.upperslaughter.co.uk) | Lower Slaughter (www.lowerslaughter.co.uk/)

5. Cleeve Hill: Free to hike. Accessible via vehicle or public transport to adjacent towns.
-Highlights: Highest peak in the Cotswolds, panoramic vistas, and diverse animals.
-Website: www.cleevecommon.org.uk

6. Painswick Rococo Garden: Entry fee applies. Accessible by vehicle or bus from Stroud.
-Highlights: Beautifully designed gardens, decorative ponds, and woodland pathways.
-Website: www.rococogarden.org.uk

7. Crickley Hill Country Park: Free access. Accessible by car or bus from Cheltenham.

-Highlights: Ancient woodlands, floral meadows, and panoramic vistas of the Severn Vale.
-Website: www.gloucestershirewildlifetrust.co.uk/nature-reserves/crickley-hill

Prepare carefully, verify local trail conditions, and start on an exciting outdoor experience in the Cotswolds.

Waterway Escapes: Canal Boating and River Cruises

Places to Go:

1. Cotswold Canals: delve into the restored waterways of the Cotswold Canals, including the Thames and Severn Canal and the Stroudwater Navigation, by renting a narrowboat or joining a guided boat excursion.

2. River Avon, Stratford-upon-Avon: Take a leisurely sail along the River Avon in Stratford-upon-Avon, passing by historic sights such as Holy Trinity Church and the Royal Shakespeare Theatre.

Highlights:

-Cotswold Canals: Highlights include sailing through stunning landscapes, going through picturesque canal locks, and viewing wildlife along the rivers.

-River Avon, Stratford-upon-Avon: Highlights include panoramic views of Stratford-upon-Avon's skyline, learning about the town's history from expert guides, and the opportunity of spotting swans and other wildlife.

Activities:

-Cotswold Canals: Rent a narrowboat for a self-directed excursion, join a guided boat tour to learn about the canal's history and ecosystem, or simply enjoy a picnic by the water.

-River Avon, Stratford-upon-Avon: Relax on a sightseeing boat while drinking refreshments, listen to comments about the river's significance to the community, and take in the vistas of historic monuments.

Pricing:

-Cotswold Canals: Narrowboat hire fees vary depending on the size of the boat and period of the rental. Guided boat excursion fees normally vary from £10 to £20 per person.

-River Avon, Stratford-upon-Avon: River cruise rates vary depending on the duration and style of voyage. Expect to pay roughly £10 to £15 for a regular sightseeing cruise.

How to Go There:

- Cotswold Canals: Various marinas and boat rental firms are located along the Cotswold Canals. Consider starting your voyage from Stroud, Saul Junction, or Ebley Wharf.

-River Avon, Stratford-upon-Avon: Stratford-upon-Avon is easily accessible by vehicle and train. Boat cruises depart from the Bancroft Gardens, located near the town center.

Websites:
-Cotswold Canals:
www.cotswoldcanals.com
-River Avon, Stratford-upon-Avon:
www.riverescapes.co.uk/stratford-upon-avon

Adrenaline Rush: Outdoor Activities for Thrill Seekers

Places to Go:

1. Cotswold Water Park: This huge area offers a range of adrenaline-pumping sports, including wakeboarding, waterskiing, and inflatable aqua parks.

2. Cotswold Edge Golf Club, Stroud: Experience the thrill of paragliding with tandem flights conducted by qualified instructors over the magnificent landscapes of the Cotswold Edge.

Highlights:

- Cotswold Water Park: Highlights include battling inflatable obstacle courses on the water, learning to wakeboard or waterski, and enjoying panoramic views from the top of a water-based climbing wall.

- Cotswold Edge Golf Club: Highlights include flying through the skies on a tandem paragliding ride, taking in aerial vistas of the Cotswold countryside, and experiencing the freedom of flight.

Activities:

- Cotswold Water Park: Try your hand at wakeboarding or water skiing with training from professional instructors, navigate through inflatable obstacle courses, and test your balance on a stand-up paddleboard.

-Cotswold Edge Golf Club: Experience the thrill of paragliding with a tandem flight supervised by a certified pilot, enjoy the sensation of soaring through the air, and capture magnificent aerial images.

Pricing:

-Cotswold Water Park: Prices vary depending on the activity and duration, with options available for single sessions, group reservations, and equipment rental. Expect to pay roughly £20 to £40 per person for most activities.

-Cotswold Edge Golf Club: Tandem paragliding flights normally cost between £100 and £150 per person, including equipment hire and instruction.

How to Go There:

-Cotswold Water Park: The water park is located near Cirencester and is easily accessible by vehicle. Parking is accessible at numerous activity locations inside the park.

-Cotswold Edge Golf Club: The club is situated near Stroud and is accessed by vehicle or public transit. Bookings for tandem paragliding flights should be made in advance.

Websites:
-Cotswold Water Park:
www.cotswoldwaterpark.com
-Cotswold Edge Golf Club:
www.cotswoldedge.co.uk

Wildlife Encounters: Birdwatching and Nature Excursions

Places to Go:

1. Slimbridge Wetland Centre: Open year-round, this natural reserve is home to a broad range of bird species, including ducks, swans, and flamingos, as well as otters and other wildlife.

2. Cotswold Falconry Centre, Moreton-in-Marsh: Experience near experiences with birds of prey through flying demonstrations, handling sessions, and hawk walks in the lovely Cotswold countryside.

Highlights:

- Slimbridge Wetland Centre: Highlights include guided birdwatching tours, viewing feeding sessions for rare and exotic species, and seeing themed exhibitions on wetland conservation.

- Cotswold Falconry Centre: Highlights include exhilarating flight demonstrations involving owls, hawks, and falcons, learning about the ancient art of falconry, and handling birds of prey under expert supervision.

Activities:

-Slimbridge Wetland Centre: Participate in birdwatching tours conducted by professional guides, try your hand at wildlife photography, and visit the Slimbridge 360 Observatory for panoramic views of the reserve.

-Cotswold Falconry Centre: Watch spectacular flight demonstrations demonstrating the agility and speed of birds of prey, handle and fly a variety of raptors, and learn about the conservation efforts to safeguard these amazing birds.

Pricing:

-Slimbridge Wetland Centre: Admission costs range from £10 to £15 for adults, with discounts for children, seniors, and families. Additional fees may apply for guided tours and special events.

- Cotswold Falconry Centre: Entry rates vary depending on the sort of experience chosen, with options available for flying displays, handling sessions, and hawk walks. Expect to pay roughly £15 to £30 per person for most activities.

How to Go There:

-Slimbridge Wetland Centre: Slimbridge is located near Dursley and is accessible by vehicle or public transit. The reserve has enough parking available for guests.

-Cotswold Falconry Centre: The center is situated near Moreton-in-Marsh and is reachable by vehicle or train. Parking is accessible on-site, and advanced booking is recommended for experiences.

Websites:
-Slimbridge Wetland Centre:
www.wwt.org.uk/wetland-centres/slimbridge
-Cotswold Falconry Centre:
www.cotswold-falconry.co.uk

CHAPTER 9:

PRACTICAL TIPS

Money Matters: Currency, Banking, and Budgeting

1. Currency: In 2024-2025, the Pound Sterling (£) remains the common currency in the UK. To prepare for your vacation, consider exchanging money into pounds or withdrawing cash from ATMs. Furthermore, many places in the UK, particularly tourist locations, accept credit and debit cards, so having one with you is helpful.

2. Banking:
- Inform your bank about your travel plans to avoid card issues while overseas.
 - Be aware of any overseas transaction fees or foreign exchange rates that your bank may levy. Consider using a card that provides good rates for foreign transactions.

3. Budgeting: Plan your budget for vacation expenses, including accommodations, transportation, food, attractions, and souvenirs.
- Determine the cost of living in the destination you're visiting. Prices may vary by area.

- Consider using budgeting apps or tools to keep track of your costs on your trip and stay within your budget.

4. Safety Tip: Avoid carrying big amounts of cash. To ensure security, utilize a combination of cash and credit cards.
   - Always keep your valuables, such as passports and credit cards, secure, especially in crowded tourist places.
   - Exercise caution when using ATMs, and choose machines in well-lit, secure areas.

5. Emergency Preparedness:
- Create a backup plan in case of lost or stolen cards. Maintain a separate cache of emergency funds in a secure area.
   - Know how to notify your bank in case your cards are lost or stolen, and keep their contact information handy.

Staying connected: Wi-Fi and mobile coverage

Staying connected when traveling is critical for navigation, communication, and accessing important information. Here's everything you need know:

1. Wi-Fi: Free Wi-Fi is available at most hotels, hostels, cafes, restaurants, and public places in popular tourist locations.

- In addition, many cities feature public Wi-Fi networks in the city center or around significant attractions.

- When utilizing public Wi-Fi, especially for sensitive activities like online banking, consider using a virtual private network (VPN) for extra security.

2. Mobile Coverage:
- The UK has considerable mobile network coverage, especially in rural regions. However, coverage quality varies by location and service provider.

- Major cities and tourist locations often have strong 4G coverage, with 5G becoming more widely available.

- To use mobile data while abroad, check with your carrier for international roaming plans or local SIM card choices. Some mobile carriers provide reasonable international roaming packages or data plans created exclusively for travelers, so check into these choices before your trip.

3. Use offline maps and apps instead of Wi-Fi or cell data for navigating.

- Apps such as Google Maps, Maps.me, and Citymapper allow users to download maps for offline usage, making navigation easier when there is no internet connection.

4. Portable Wi-Fi Devices: If you expect to need continuous internet connectivity while traveling, consider renting a portable Wi-Fi device, commonly known as a pocket Wi-Fi or MiFi. These gadgets function as a personal Wi-Fi hotspot, allowing you to connect several devices.

Health and Safety: Important Precautions and Emergency Contacts

Taking required precautions and being prepared for emergencies are essential for ensuring one's health and safety while traveling. Here are some important guidelines and emergency contacts for travelers in 2024-2025:

1. Precautions:
- Research health risks and vaccines for your trip and check with a healthcare expert before travel.
   - Bring a travel health pack containing medications, first aid supplies, hand sanitizer, and any necessary prescriptions.
   - Stay hydrated, eat well, and get enough sleep to keep your immune system healthy when traveling.

- Maintain good hygiene by often handwashing and using hand sanitizer, especially before eating or touching your face.

- To avoid foodborne infections, practice food and water safety and only consume from trustworthy sources.

2. Emergency Contacts:

-Emergency Services: In the UK, call 999 for police, fire, or ambulance assistance.

- Non-Emergency Medical Assistance: In the UK, contact 111 for medical advice and assistance if your medical condition is not life-threatening.

-Embassy or Consulate: Have the contact information for your country's embassy or consulate in case of passport loss, legal concerns, or other circumstances that necessitate assistance from your home country's authorities.

-Travel Insurance Provider: Keep a copy of your travel insurance policy and your insurance provider's emergency contact information close to hand. In the event of a medical emergency, an accident, or a travel disruption, call your insurance provider for help and advice.

3. Safety Tips:
- Stay educated about local safety and security conditions in your destination, and follow any travel advisories or cautions issued by the authorities.
- Keep your valuables secure and be mindful of your surroundings, particularly in crowded or touristy places where pickpocketing and theft are common.
   - Share your itinerary and contact information with a trusted person back home, and check in on a frequent basis to keep them up to date on your location.
   - Familiarize yourself with local laws, customs, and cultural norms to prevent accidentally offending or disobeying the regulations.

Travelers can assist guarantee their health and safety while on the road by taking these steps and having emergency contact information.

Sustainable Travel: Environmentally Friendly Practices and Responsible Tourism

Promoting sustainable travel and responsible tourism practices is critical to reducing environmental impact and maintaining locations for future generations. Here are some eco-friendly practices and responsible tourism ideas for travelers:

1. Choose Eco-Friendly Accommodations:
- Look for hotels, hostels, or eco-lodges that use sustainable techniques including energy and water conservation, waste reduction, and renewable resources.
- Look for certifications such as LEED (Leadership in Energy and Environmental Design) or Green Key to find ecologically friendly hotels.

2. Reduce Carbon Footprint:
- Use alternative modes of transportation, such as trains or buses, instead of flying.
   - If flying is necessary, explore carbon offset programs to reduce the environmental impact of your flights.

3. Conserve Resources:
  - Reduce water and energy consumption by taking shorter showers, turning off lights and air conditioning, and reusing towels and linens.
   - Minimize plastic waste by carrying a reusable water bottle, shopping bag, and utensils, and avoid single-use plastics whenever possible.

4. Support Local Communities:
- Choose locally-owned accommodations, restaurants, and tour operators to benefit the local economy and reduce the carbon imprint of international enterprises.

- Respect local customs, traditions, and cultures, and interact with local populations in a meaningful and respectful way.

5. Reduce Waste:
- Dispose of waste responsibly through recycling, composting, or following local requirements.
- Instead of buying souvenirs created from endangered species or unsustainable materials, choose locally made things that benefit local artisans and craftspeople.

6. Leave No Trace:
When visiting natural places, follow Leave No Trace principles by staying on established routes, removing garbage, and avoiding harming wildlife or ecosystems.

7. Educate Yourself and Others:
Learn about environmental and cultural challenges in the areas you visit, and share your knowledge with other tourists to promote responsible conduct.

By following these eco-friendly practices and responsible tourism principles, tourists can reduce their environmental effect while also contributing to the protection of locations across the world.

Further Reading

Here are some resources for further reading, specifically suited to first-time visitors to the Cotswolds region.

1. Books:
-Richard Churchley's "Cotswolds: A Cultural History" and Caroline Mills' "Slow Cotswolds: Local, Characterful Guides to Britain's Special Places".
-"Walking in the Cotswolds: 30 Classic Hill and Valley Routes" by Damian Hall

2. Websites and Blogs:
-Cotswolds.com (https://www.cotswolds.com/) is the official tourism website for the Cotswolds, providing detailed information on attractions, lodgings, events, and more.
- The Cotswolds Conservation Board (https://www.cotswoldsaonb.org.uk/) provides information on conservation efforts, outdoor activities, and sustainable tourism practices in the Area of Outstanding Natural Beauty.
-CotswoldsInfo.net (https://www.cotswoldsinfo.net/) - Provides travel guides, itinerary ideas, and practical advice for touring the Cotswolds.

3. Online Articles:

- 10 Must-Visit Villages in the Cotswolds: Guide to the region's most gorgeous and charming settlements.
 - Outdoor Adventures in the Cotswolds: Exploring Nature's Playground
- Emphasizes outdoor activities including hiking, cycling, and wildlife viewing in the Cotswold countryside.

4. Local Events and Festivals
- Keep a look out for local events, festivals, and markets during your visit to get a sense of the Cotswolds' lively culture and community spirit.

These materials will assist first-time visitors to obtain a better understanding of the Cotswolds region, organize their itinerary, and make the most of their stay in this lovely and peaceful area of England.

CHAPTER 10:

3-DAY TAILORED ITINERARIES

The History Buff's Retreat

Day 1: Journey Through Time at Stow-on-the-Wold and Chipping Campden
- Morning: Start your day with a guided walking tour of Stow-on-the-Wold, a market town with a rich history reaching back to the medieval period. Explore the ancient market square, visit St. Edward's Church, and learn about the town's role during the English Civil War.

- Afternoon: Head to Chipping Campden, noted for its well-preserved limestone structures and ancient market hall. Visit the 17th-century almshouses, wander along the lovely High Street, and admire the architecture of the Woolstaplers Hall.

Day 2: Royal Residences and Monastic Ruins
- Morning: Explore Sudeley Castle, a beautiful Tudor castle with royal links, including Queen Katherine Parr's ultimate resting place. Discover its gorgeous gardens, displays, and historical treasures.

- Afternoon: Visit Hailes Abbey, a quiet Cistercian abbey dating back to the 13th century. Explore the ruins and learn about the abbey's intriguing history, including its connection to the Magna Carta.

Day 3: Roman Heritage and Wildlife Encounters
- Morning: Immerse yourself in Roman history at the Corinium Museum in Cirencester. Discover items from the Roman conquest of Britain and learn about life in the ancient city of Corinium Dobunnorum.

-Afternoon: Spend the day visiting Cotswold Wildlife Park, where you may encounter a wide assortment of exotic creatures from throughout the world. Enjoy feeding sessions, animal encounters, and picturesque walks around the park's beautifully landscaped grounds.

Adventure seeker

Day 1: Adrenaline Rush
Morning:
- Start your day with a thrilling paragliding experience over the rolling hills of the Cotswolds.
- Head to the closeby town of Cheltenham for a hearty breakfast at a local cafe.

Afternoon:

- Go on a rock climbing adventure at Symonds Yat Rock, known for its challenging limestone cliffs and stunning views of the River Wye.
- Savor a picnic lunch overlooking the river before continuing your adventure.

Evening:
- Return to Cheltenham and relax with a delicious dinner at a cozy pub, sharing stories of your day's adrenaline-fueled activities.

Day 2: Nature Exploration
Morning:
- Begin your day with a sunrise hot air balloon ride over the picturesque Cotswold countryside, taking in breathtaking views of the landscape below.
- After your flight, savor a delicious breakfast at a local farmhouse or inn.

Afternoon:
- Spend the afternoon traversing the underground world of the Cotswold caves with a guided caving expedition.
- Discover hidden chambers, underground rivers, and fascinating rock formations as you navigate through the subterranean labyrinth.

Evening:

- After emerging from the caves, relax and rejuvenate with a leisurely dinner at a countryside restaurant, enjoying local delicacies and reflecting on your day of adventure.

Day 3: Water Adventures

Morning:
- Kick off your day with an adrenaline-pumping kayaking adventure along the River Thames or the River Avon, depending on your preference.
- Navigate gentle rapids, traverse tranquil stretches of water, and immerse in the natural beauty of the Cotswold waterways.

Afternoon:
- After lunch, switch gears and try your hand at stand-up paddleboarding on one of the Cotswold's serene lakes or reservoirs.
- Savor the peacefulness of gliding across the water, surrounded by lush greenery and wildlife.

Evening:
- Conclude your adventure-filled day with a relaxing evening at a lakeside campsite, where you can unwind by the fire, stargaze, and share tales of your waterborne stories with fellow adventurers.

Honeymoon Couples Escape

Day 1: Romantic Retreat
Morning:
- Begin your day with a leisurely breakfast in bed at a cozy bed and breakfast or luxury boutique hotel in one of the Cotswold's charming villages.
- Take a romantic stroll hand in hand through the picturesque streets, savoring the honey-colored cottages and quaint shops.

Afternoon:
- Immerse in a couples spa experience at a luxury spa resort, where you can relax and unwind with massages, facials, and other pampering treatments.
- After your spa session, enjoy a romantic picnic lunch in a scenic spot overlooking the countryside.

Evening:
- Dine at a candlelit restaurant specializing in fine Cotswold cuisine, savoring each bite and toasting to your love with a glass of local wine or champagne.

Day 2: Love in Bloom
Morning:
- Start your day with a visit to one of the Cotswold's beautiful gardens, such as Hidcote Manor Garden or Painswick Rococo Garden.

- Wander hand in hand through the colorful blooms, stopping to smell the roses and admire the serene environment.

Afternoon:
- Enjoy a couples countryside drive, stopping at charming villages along the way to traverse local shops and galleries.
- Surprise your partner with a hot air balloon ride over the Cotswold countryside, taking in panoramic views of the landscape below.

Evening:
- Return to your accommodation for a private candlelit dinner, set by the hotel staff, either in your room or in a secluded garden setting.

Day 3: Adventure and Romance
Morning:
- Start your day with a sunrise hot air balloon ride over the picturesque Cotswold countryside, taking in breathtaking views of the landscape below.
- After your flight, enjoy a champagne breakfast served onboard the balloon or at a nearby cafe.

Afternoon:
- Spend the afternoon exploring a romantic castle or historic estate, such as Sudeley Castle or Blenheim

Palace, where you can stroll through breathtaking gardens and admire stunning architecture.
- Enjoy a romantic picnic lunch on the grounds of the castle or estate, surrounded by history and natural beauty.

Evening:
- Roundup your romantic getaway with a private sunset cruise along the River Avon, sipping champagne and watching the sun dip below the horizon as you reflect on your memorable honeymoon in the Cotswolds.

Luxury Seekers

Day 1: Indulgent Relaxation
Morning:
- Arrive at your luxury accommodation, whether it's a stately manor, boutique hotel, or exclusive countryside retreat.
- Savor a leisurely breakfast served in your room or at the hotel's fine dining restaurant.

Afternoon:
- Treat yourself to a pampering spa experience at the hotel's luxurious spa facilities, indulging in massages, facials, and other rejuvenating treatments.

- After your spa session, relax by the hotel's pool or in a private hot tub, soaking in the serene surroundings.

Evening:
- Dine at the hotel's Michelin-starred restaurant, enjoying gourmet cuisine prepared with locally sourced ingredients and paired with fine wines from the region's vineyards.

Day 2: Exclusive Experiences
Morning:
- After a sumptuous breakfast, embark on a private tour of a closeby historic estate or castle, led by a knowledgeable guide who will share insights into the region's rich history and heritage.
- Tour the estate's beautiful gardens, art collections, and architectural marvels at your own pace.

Afternoon:
- Enjoy a custom culinary experience, such as a private cooking class with a known local chef, where you can learn to prepare traditional Cotswold dishes using the freshest seasonal ingredients.
- Indulge in a gourmet lunch featuring the dishes you've prepared, paired with fine wines selected by the chef.

Evening:

- Return to your accommodation for a romantic candlelit dinner, served in a private dining room or alfresco on a terrace overlooking the countryside, roundup with personalized service and attention to detail.

Day 3: Opulent Adventures
Morning:
- Begin your day with a hot air balloon ride over the picturesque Cotswold countryside, enjoying beautiful views of rolling hills, lush valleys, and quaint villages below.
- Upon landing, enjoy a champagne breakfast served at a scenic location, surrounded by the awe of the countryside.

Afternoon:
- Spend the afternoon immersing in luxury shopping at the Cotswold's upscale boutiques, art galleries, and artisan shops, where you can find unique treasures and souvenirs to remember your trip.
- Treat yourself to a private wine tasting experience at a local vineyard, sampling premium wines accompanied by gourmet cheese and charcuterie.

Evening:
- Complete your luxurious getaway with a private sunset helicopter tour over the Cotswold countryside, providing

breathtaking views of the landscape bathed in golden light.
- Return to your accommodation for a final night of relaxation and immersion, savoring every moment of your unforgettable luxury experience in the Cotswolds.

Family-friendly Getaway

Day 1: Outdoor Adventures
Morning:
- Begin your day with a visit to Cotswold Wildlife Park and Gardens, where the whole family can savor seeing exotic animals and exploring beautifully landscaped gardens.
- Have a picnic lunch in the park or enjoy a meal at the on-site cafe.

Afternoon:
- Head to the Cotswold Water Park for an afternoon of family-friendly water sports and activities. Options include kayaking, paddleboarding, and inflatable obstacle courses.
- Savor ice cream by the lake before heading back to your accommodation.

Evening:

- Return to your accommodation for a relaxed family dinner, either at a local restaurant or by cooking a meal together in your holiday rental.

Day 2: Cultural Exploration
Morning:
- Explore the historic town of Stratford-upon-Avon, birthplace of William Shakespeare. Visit Shakespeare's Birthplace, Anne Hathaway's Cottage, and other landmarks associated with the famous playwright.
- Have lunch at a family-friendly restaurant in town.

Afternoon:
- Spend the afternoon at the Cotswold Motoring Museum and Toy Collection in Bourton-on-the-Water, where kids can marvel at vintage cars and toy displays.
- Take a leisurely stroll along the river and let the kids feed the ducks.

Evening:
- Savor a relaxed dinner at a family-friendly pub in Bourton-on-the-Water, soaking in the village atmosphere.

Day 3: Nature and Fun
Morning:

- Visit the Cotswold Farm Park, where kids can interact with farm animals, enjoy tractor rides, and play in the adventure playground.
- Have lunch at the farm's cafe, featuring locally sourced ingredients.

Afternoon:
- Spend the afternoon at Cotswold Country Park and Beach, where the family can enjoy sandcastle building, pedal boating, and lakeside walks.
- Treat the kids to ice cream or snacks from the park's cafe.

Evening:
- Complete your family-friendly getaway with a relaxed dinner at your accommodation, reminiscing about the fun adventures you've had together in the Cotswolds.

Budget Traveler

Day 1: Countryside Charm
Morning:
- Start your day with a visit to Bibury, one of the Cotswolds' most picturesque villages known for its Arlington Row cottages.
- Take a leisurely stroll along the River Coln and traverse the village's historic sites.

Afternoon:
- Pack a picnic lunch and head to Cirencester, a beautiful market town with plenty of green spaces. Enjoy your meal in Abbey Grounds or Cirencester Park.

Evening:
- Dine at a budget-friendly pub or cafe in Cirencester, sampling traditional British fare without breaking the bank.

Day 2: Historic Exploration
Morning:
- Explore the historic town of Burford, often referred to as the 'Gateway to the Cotswolds.' Wander along its High Street and explore St John the Baptist Church.

Afternoon:
- Visit Chedworth Roman Villa, an English Heritage site offering a glimpse into Roman life in the Cotswolds. Entry fees are typically cheap, especially for families.

Evening:
- Opt for a self-catered dinner using local produce from a farmers' market or grocery store, enjoying a meal in your accommodation's kitchen or a nearby picnic spot.

Day 3: Outdoor Adventure

Morning:
- Start your day with a hike along a section of the Cotswold Way, a long-distance footpath providing stunning views of the countryside. Pack a picnic to enjoy along the way.

Afternoon:
- Visit the Rollright Stones, a prehistoric stone circle surrounded by myths and legends. Entry is usually free, allowing you to tour the site at your own pace.

Evening:
- complete your budget-friendly adventure with a meal at a local takeaway or street food vendor, indulging in delicious eats without breaking the bank. Alternatively, consider cooking a simple meal with ingredients from a budget supermarket.

Solo Traveler

Day 1: Exploring Charming Villages
Morning:
- Commence your day by exploring the charming village of Bourton-on-the-Water, often called the "Venice of the Cotswolds." Stroll along the river, visit the Model Village, and explore the quirky shops.

Afternoon:
- Head to Stow-on-the-Wold, another picturesque Cotswold village. Wander through the historic streets, visit the market square, and explore the local boutiques and antique shops.

Evening:
- Enjoy a solo dinner at a cozy pub or restaurant in Stow-on-the-Wold, where you can sample traditional Cotswold cuisine and perhaps strike up a conversation with locals or fellow travelers.

Day 2: Nature and History
Morning:
- Spend the morning hiking or cycling along a section of the Cotswold Way, enjoying the scenic views and peaceful countryside. Pack a picnic to savor at a scenic spot along the trail.

Afternoon:
- Visit one of the Cotswolds' historic sites, such as Sudeley Castle or Hailes Abbey. Tour the grounds, learn about the area's rich history, and take in the beautiful architecture.

Evening:

- Treat yourself to a solo dinner at a casual restaurant or cafe in a nearby town, reflecting on the day's adventures and planning for the days ahead.

Day 3: Tranquil Retreat
Morning:
- Start your day with a visit to Westonbirt Arboretum, home to thousands of trees and shrubs from around the world. Take a peaceful stroll through the arboretum's paths and enjoy the tranquility of nature.

Afternoon:
- Spend the afternoon at a local spa or wellness center, indulging in a massage or other pampering treatments. Alternatively, visit a closeby garden or park for a relaxing afternoon picnic or leisurely walk.

Evening:
- Finalize your solo adventure with a quiet dinner at your accommodation or a nearby restaurant, savoring the flavors of the Cotswolds and reflecting on your solo journey through this beautiful region.

CHAPTER 11:

BEYOND COTSWOLDS

Day Trips and Excursions: Nearby Attractions and Hidden Gems

Here's the updated concepts with highlights for each destination:

1. Blenheim Palace:
-Highlights: Discover the amazing Baroque architecture, visit the palace, its exquisite gardens, and the adjacent parkland.

- How to Get There: Blenheim Palace is located near Woodstock in Oxfordshire, about a 1-hour drive from the Cotswolds. There are other bus services available from Oxford.
-Website: www.blenheimpalace.com

2. The Malvern Hills:
 -Highlights: Enjoy stunning views and good hiking possibilities, including ascending Worcestershire Beacon for panoramic vistas.

-How to Get There: The Malvern Hills are roughly a 1.5-hour journey from the Cotswolds. There are other rail services from Moreton-in-Marsh or Kingham stations to Great Malvern station, with a journey time of roughly 2 hours.
-Website: www.malvernhills.org.uk

3. Bristol:
-Highlights: Visit the SS Great Britain, Bristol Zoo Gardens, and the Clifton Suspension Bridge in this dynamic city with a strong maritime heritage.

-How to Get There: Bristol is approximately a 1.5-hour journey from the Cotswolds. You can alternatively catch a train from Moreton-in-Marsh or Kemble stations, with a journey time of roughly 1.5 to 2 hours.
-Website: https://visitbristol.co.uk

5. Gloucester:
-Highlights: Explore the ancient docks, Gloucester Cathedral, and learn the city's Roman beginnings at the Museum of Gloucester.

-How to Get There: Gloucester is about a 45-minute drive from the Cotswolds. Train services from Moreton-in-Marsh or Kemble stations to Gloucester take roughly 30-40 minutes.
-Website: www.visitgloucester.co.uk

6. Cheltenham:

-Highlights: Visit the Pittville Pump Room, Cheltenham Racecourse, and experience cultural festivals in this town noted for its Regency architecture.

-How to Get There: Cheltenham is approximately a 30 to 45-minute drive from the Cotswolds. You can alternatively take a train from Moreton-in-Marsh or Kingham stations to Cheltenham Spa station, with a journey time of roughly 20-30 minutes.
-Website: www.visitcheltenham.com

These highlights provide a look into the unique experiences and attractions each destination has to offer, assuring a delightful day trip or excursion beyond the Cotswolds.

Exploring Nearby Cities: Oxford, Bath, and Stratford-upon-Avon

Exploring adjacent cities like Oxford, Bath, and Stratford-upon-Avon gives a deeper dig into England's rich history, culture, and architecture:

1. Oxford:

-Highlights: Wander through the medieval colleges of Oxford University, see the Bodleian Library, climb the tower of the University Church of St. Mary the Virgin for panoramic views, and stroll around the gorgeous Oxford Botanic Garden.

- How to Get There: Oxford is about a 1-hour drive from the Cotswolds. Trains from Moreton-in-Marsh or Kingham stations to Oxford take around 40-50 minutes.
-Website: www.visitoxford.org

2. Bath:
-Highlights: Explore the well-preserved Roman Baths, marvel at the Georgian architecture of the Royal Crescent and the Circus, see Bath Abbey, and relax in the Thermae Bath Spa for a modern take on historic thermal baths.

-How to Get There: Bath is approximately a 1.5 to 2-hour drive from the Cotswolds. You can alternatively take a direct train from Moreton-in-Marsh or Kemble stations, with a journey time of roughly 1.5 to 2 hours.
-Website: https://visitbath.co.uk

3. Stratford-upon-Avon:
-Highlights: Immerse yourself in the world of William Shakespeare by visiting his birthplace, Anne Hathaway's Cottage, and the Royal Shakespeare Theatre. Take a

leisurely stroll along the River Avon and discover the lovely lanes lined with Tudor-style architecture.

-How to Get There: From the Cotswolds, Stratford-upon-Avon is easily accessible by automobile, around a 1-hour trip. Alternatively, you can take a train from Moreton-in-Marsh station, with a journey duration of roughly 30-40 minutes.
-Websitem: Shakespeare's England: www.shakespeares-england.co.uk

These cities offer a blend of historic landmarks, cultural attractions, and scenic beauty, delivering an engaging experience beyond just a day vacation. Each destination has its own particular charm and attractions waiting to be explored.

Extended Adventures: Planning Your Next Journey from Cotswolds

Planning an extended adventure from the Cotswolds throws up a world of possibilities. Here are some options for your next journey:

1. Lake District National Park:

-Highlights: Explore magnificent lakes, mountains, and lovely villages. Enjoy outdoor activities such as hiking, boating, and wildlife spotting.

-How to Get There: The Lake District is around a 4 to 5-hour trip from the Cotswolds. Alternatively, you can take a train to places like Windermere or Penrith, with a journey time of roughly 4 to 5 hours.
-Website: www.lakedistrict.gov.uk

2. Scottish Highlands:
-Highlights: Discover rough scenery, medieval castles, and lonely lochs. Experience Scottish culture, whisky distilleries, and outdoor adventures like hiking and animal watching.

-How to Get There: The Scottish Highlands are around a 7 to 8-hour journey from the Cotswolds. Alternatively, you can take a train to cities like Inverness or Fort William, with journey times of roughly 7 to 8 hours.
-Website:
www.visitscotland.com/destinations-maps/highlands

3. Cornwall:
-Highlights: Enjoy spectacular coastal scenery, sandy beaches, and picturesque fishing communities. Visit historic landmarks including Tintagel Castle and the Eden Project.

-How to Get There: Cornwall is about a 3 to 4-hour journey from the Cotswolds. You can also take a train to places like Penzance or St. Austell, with a journey time of roughly 4 to 5 hours.
-Website: www.visitcornwall.com

4. Peak District National Park:
-Highlights: Experience spectacular vistas, limestone valleys, and old settlements. Enjoy outdoor activities such as hiking, cycling, and rock climbing.

-How to Get There: The Peak District is around a 2 to 3-hour journey from the Cotswolds. Alternatively, you can take a train to locations like Sheffield or Derby, with a journey time of roughly 2 to 3 hours.
-Website: www.peakdistrict.gov.uk

5. Jurassic Coast:
-Highlights: Discover spectacular coastal landscapes, fossil-rich cliffs, and unusual geological formations. Visit lovely towns like Lyme Regis and enjoy the natural splendor of areas like Durdle Door and Lulworth Cove.

-How to Get There: The Jurassic Coast is about a 3 to 4-hour journey from the Cotswolds. You can also take a rail to places like Dorchester or Weymouth, with a journey time of roughly 3 to 4 hours.

-Website: https://jurassiccoast.org

These extended adventures provide different experiences, from outdoor adventures to cultural exploration, assuring an enjoyable voyage from the Cotswolds.

CHAPTER 12:

SHOPPING & SOUVENIRS

Unique Boutiques & Antique Stores

1. Cotswold Trading (Stow-on-the-Wold):
This store offers a chosen variety of homeware, gifts, and accessories inspired by the Cotswold region. Visitors can find finely crafted ceramics, sumptuous linens, and handcrafted skincare products, perfect for bringing a touch of the Cotswolds into their homes.

-How to get there: Located in the heart of Stow-on-the-Wold, Cotswold Trading is easily accessible by car or public transit. Visitors can take a train to Moreton-in-Marsh station and then a short taxi ride to Stow-on-the-Wold.
-Website: www.cotswoldtrading.com

2. Emma Bridgewater Factory (Stoke-on-Trent): While not in the Cotswolds itself, the Emma Bridgewater Factory is a must-visit for pottery enthusiasts. Here, visitors may experience the traditional workmanship behind the distinctive hand-painted ceramics, including mugs, plates, and kitchenware. The factory shop offers a

wide choice of exclusive designs, making it a great location for unique mementos.

-How to get there: Visitors can drive to Stoke-on-Trent or take a train to Stoke-on-Trent station, followed by a short cab ride to the Emma Bridgewater Factory.
-Website: www.emmabridgewater.co.uk

3. The Cotswold Perfumery (Bourton-on-the-Water): Perfume connoisseurs will revel in a visit to The Cotswold Perfumery, where they can discover an array of unique perfumes inspired by the natural beauty of the Cotswold landscape. Visitors can visit the perfume museum, learn about the art of perfume-making, and even create their own bespoke fragrance during a guided workshop.

-How to get there: Situated in Bourton-on-the-Water, The Cotswold Perfumery is easily accessible by vehicle or public transit.
-Website: www.cotswold-perfumery.co.uk

4. Lorfords Antiques & Interiors (Tetbury): Another haven for antique collectors, Lorfords Antiques & Interiors offers a huge selection of rare furniture, decorative artifacts, and artworks gathered from merchants across the Cotswolds and beyond. Housed in a historic warehouse, this store is a treasure trove of

vintage finds, from rustic farmhouse pieces to elegant period furniture. Visitors can tour the showroom's handpicked displays and uncover timeless treasures to beautify their homes.

-How to get there: Located in Tetbury, a lovely market town in the Cotswolds. Visitors can drive to Tetbury or take a rail to Kemble station, followed by a short cab ride to Tetbury.
-Website: www.lorfordsantiques.com

5. Wildwood Antiques (Stow-on-the-Wold): Situated in the heart of Stow-on-the-Wold, Wildwood Antiques offers a handpicked variety of beautiful antiques, vintage furniture, and decorative goods. Housed in a historic structure, this boutique emanates charm and character, presenting guests with a glimpse into the past. From elegant Georgian items to rustic farmhouse finds, Wildwood Antiques exhibits a broad assortment of treasures waiting to be unearthed.

-How to get there: Located on Stow-on-the-Wold, making it conveniently accessible by vehicle or public transit.
-Website: www.wildwoodantiques.co.uk

Local Products to Bring Home

1. Artisanal Cheeses: Explore farmers' markets or specialty cheese shops like The Cotswold Cheese Company(https://www.cotswoldcheese.com/) in Moreton-in-Marsh. Prices vary based on the type and quantity, but expect to pay roughly £5-£10 per cheese.

2. Cotswold honey: Purchase jars of raw, unfiltered honey from local farm shops or beekeepers' stalls at markets like the Stroud Farmers' Market (https://fresh-n-local.co.uk/markets/stroud/). Prices range from £5-£15 per jar, depending on size and variety.

3. Handcrafted pottery: Visit pottery workshops in locations like Winchcombe or Chipping Campden, or browse shops like The Pottery Place (www.thepotteryplace.co.uk/) in Burford. Prices for clay pieces range from £10 for tiny objects to £100 or more for larger pieces.

4. Jams and preserves: Find a range of flavors in farm shops, specialty food stores, or markets like the Bourton-on-the-Water Farmers' Market (https://www.bourtoninfo.com/market.htm). Prices typically range from £3-£8 per jar.

5. Cotswold woolens: Look for locally-made blankets, scarves, and throws at businesses like Cotswold Woollen Weavers (www.cotswoldwoollenweavers.co.uk/) in Filkins. Prices vary based on size and material, but expect to pay roughly £30-£100 for a decent woolen piece.

6. Lavender products: Visit lavender farms such as Cotswold Lavender (www.cotswoldlavender.co.uk/) in Snowshill, where you can purchase lavender-scented soaps, candles, and sachets. Prices range from £5-£20 depending on the item.

7. Farm-fresh produce: Browse farmers' markets such as the Tetbury Market (https://www.visittetbury.co.uk/events/tetbury-market) or Cirencester Farmers' Market (https://www.cirencester.gov.uk/markets) for seasonal fruits, veggies, and artisanal breads. Prices vary depending on the product and vendor.

8. Cotswold gin: Visit distilleries like Cotswolds Distillery (https://www.cotswoldsdistillery.com/) in Shipston-on-Stour for craft gin blended with botanicals from the region. Prices typically range from £30-£50 per bottle.

9. Cotswold chocolate: Find handmade chocolates blended with locally-inspired flavors at specialized chocolate stores like The Chocolate Tart (https://thechocolatetart.co.uk/) in Chipping Norton. Prices vary based on the type and quantity of chocolate, but expect to pay roughly £5-£15 for a box of chocolates.

CHAPTER 13:

CLOSING THOUGHTS

Tips for Preserving Memories and Sharing Your Stories

As your Cotswolds experience draws to a conclusion, I urge you to keep onto those moments that have woven themselves into the fabric of your soul. As you stand amidst the rolling hills and watch the sun fall below the horizon, let the warmth of these memories wrap around you like a soothing embrace.

When you return home, don't allow those cherished memories to go away with the passing of time. Instead, find ways to keep them alive in your everyday life. Whether it's through producing a scrapbook packed with pressed wildflowers obtained from the countryside or framing a favorite photograph of a gorgeous village, find a physical way to hold onto the pleasure of your journey.

And most importantly, share your tales with people closest to you. Pour a cup of tea, gather around the fireplace, and regale your friends and family with tales of beautiful interactions with locals, leisurely stroll through historic forests, and the simple satisfaction of savoring a typical English cream tea.

In doing so, you'll not only preserve the memories of your Cotswolds experience but also inspire others to seek out their own moments of serenity and beauty in this big and amazing globe.

Farewell to Cotswolds: Until We Meet Again

As the sun sets on my stay in the Cotswolds, I can't help but feel a twinge of melancholy knowing that my journey through this gorgeous region must come to an end. Yet, when I bid farewell to the rolling hills and picturesque villages, I take solace in knowing that this is not goodbye, but rather, a "see you later."

Until we meet again, Cotswolds, I'll cherish the memories of your charming towns and lush greenery in my heart. Your serene beauty has left an everlasting impact on my soul, and I know that I'll wish to return to your embrace time and time again.

As I return home, I'll cherish the moments we shared—the laughter of new friendships established in warm pubs, the peacefulness of early morning walks across dew-kissed meadows, and the simple joy of slowing down and relishing each moment.

So, farewell for now, lovely Cotswolds. But rest assured, our paths will cross again, and until then, I'll hang onto the enchantment of our time together, allowing it to lead me through the voyage ahead.

ACKNOWLEDGEMENT

Special Thanks to the Locals, Experts and Contributors

I wish to convey my heartfelt gratitude to the people, specialists, and contributors who made my vacation to the Cotswolds an amazing experience. Your warmth, hospitality, and abundance of knowledge brought layers of richness to my voyage through this gorgeous region.

To the residents who opened their doors and shared their stories, thank you for welcoming me into your towns with open arms. Your sincere politeness and commitment for conserving the beauty of the Cotswolds left a lasting impression on me.

To the specialists who escorted me through hidden gems and historical treasures, thank you for highlighting the wonderful history and culture of this enchanting area. Your views and knowledge increased my understanding and admiration of the Cotswolds.

And to all the contributors—whether artisans crafting exquisite local products, storytellers sharing tales of bygone eras, or conservationists working relentlessly to protect the natural beauty of the landscape—thank you for all you do to contribute to preserving the magic of the Cotswolds for generations to come.

Your collaborative efforts have left an everlasting stamp on my heart, and I am genuinely grateful for the memories we created together. Until we meet again, may the spirit of the Cotswolds continue to thrive, guided by the enthusiasm and generosity of its people.

Printed in Great Britain
by Amazon